Untamed Ocean Coloring Book by Kristy Specht

ISBN-13: 978-0692886700 (Kristy J. Specht)
ISBN-10: 0692886702

INSTAGRAM @ THEECOMICALARTIST
FACEBOOK: HTTPS://WWW.FACEBOOK.COM/THEECOMICALARTIST

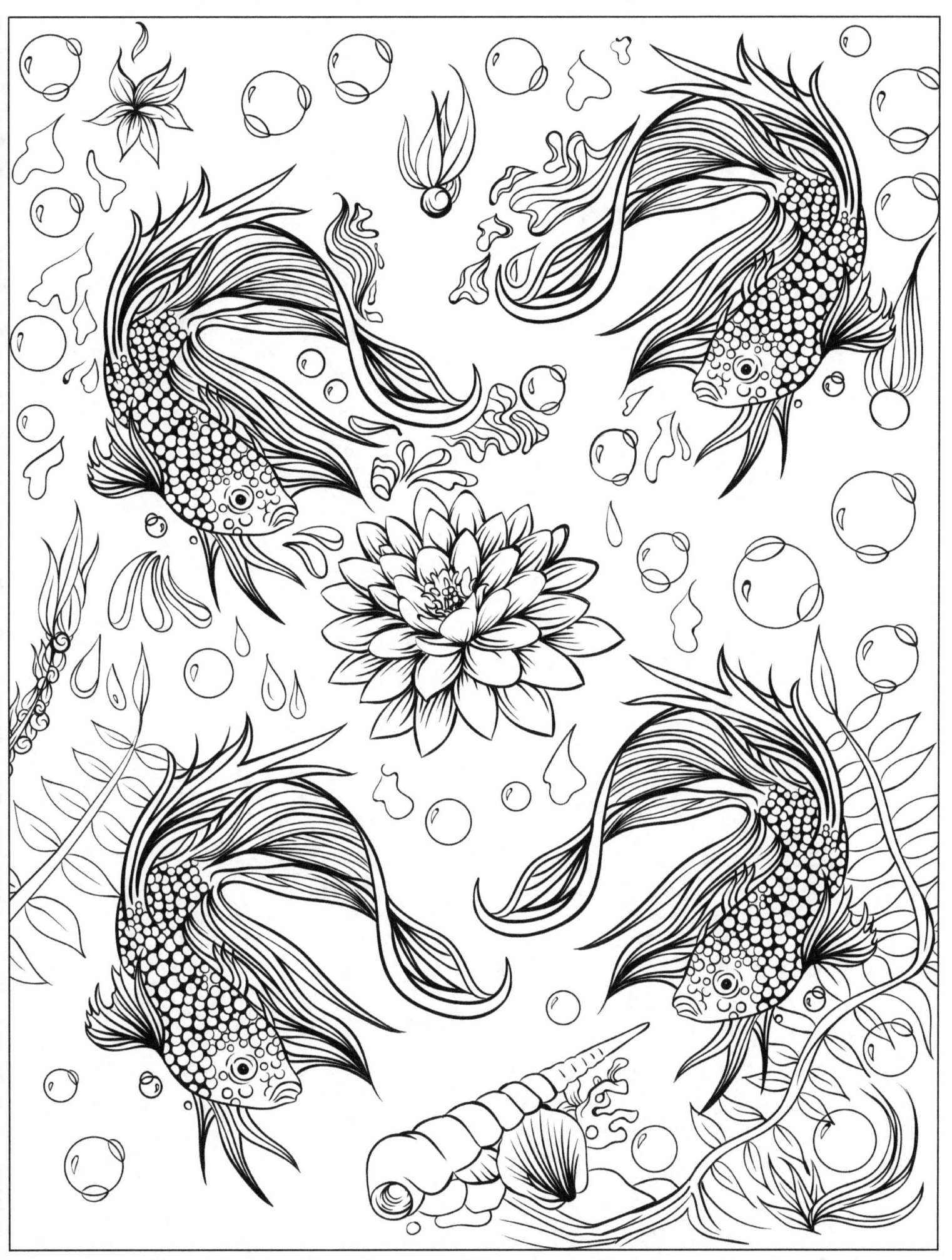

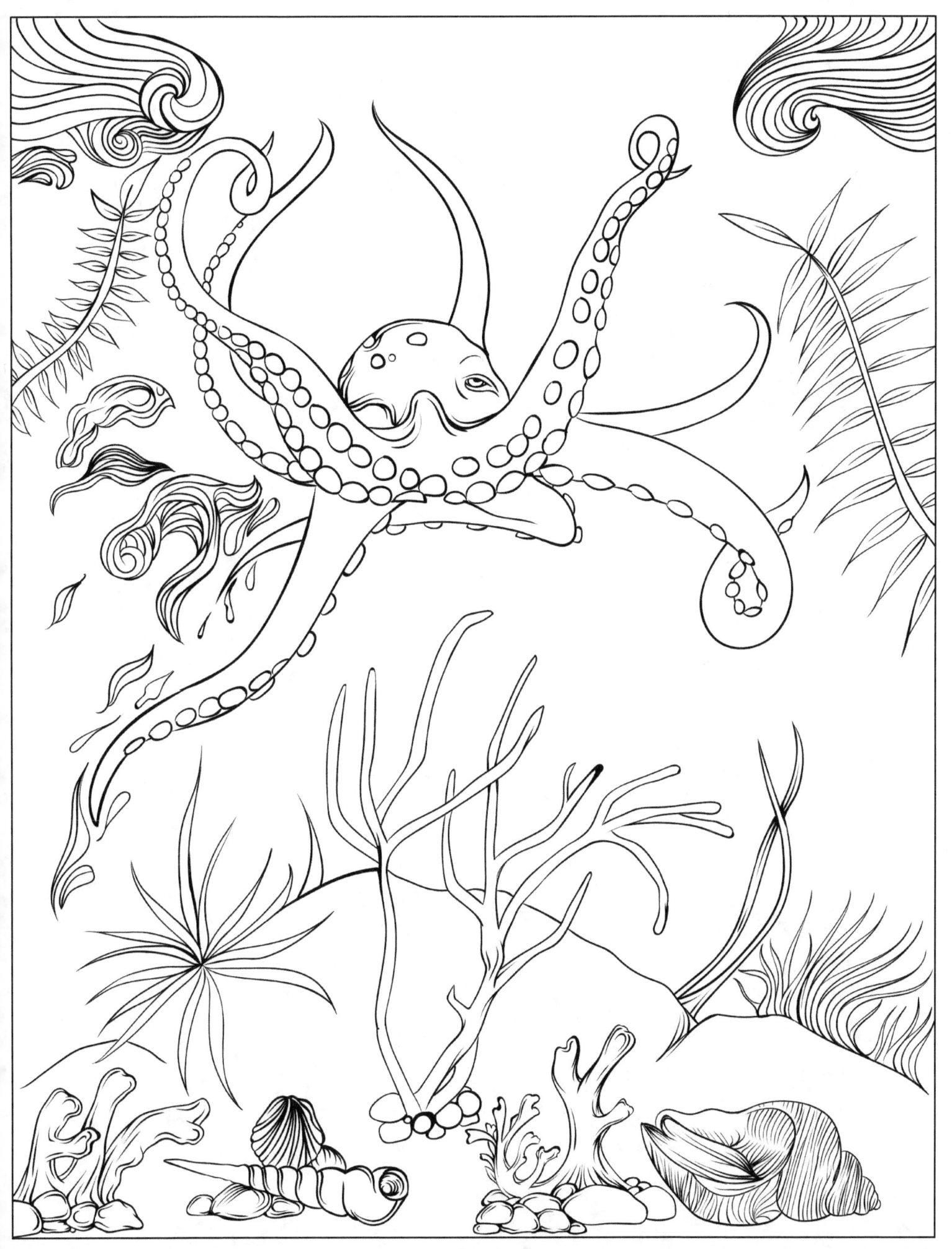

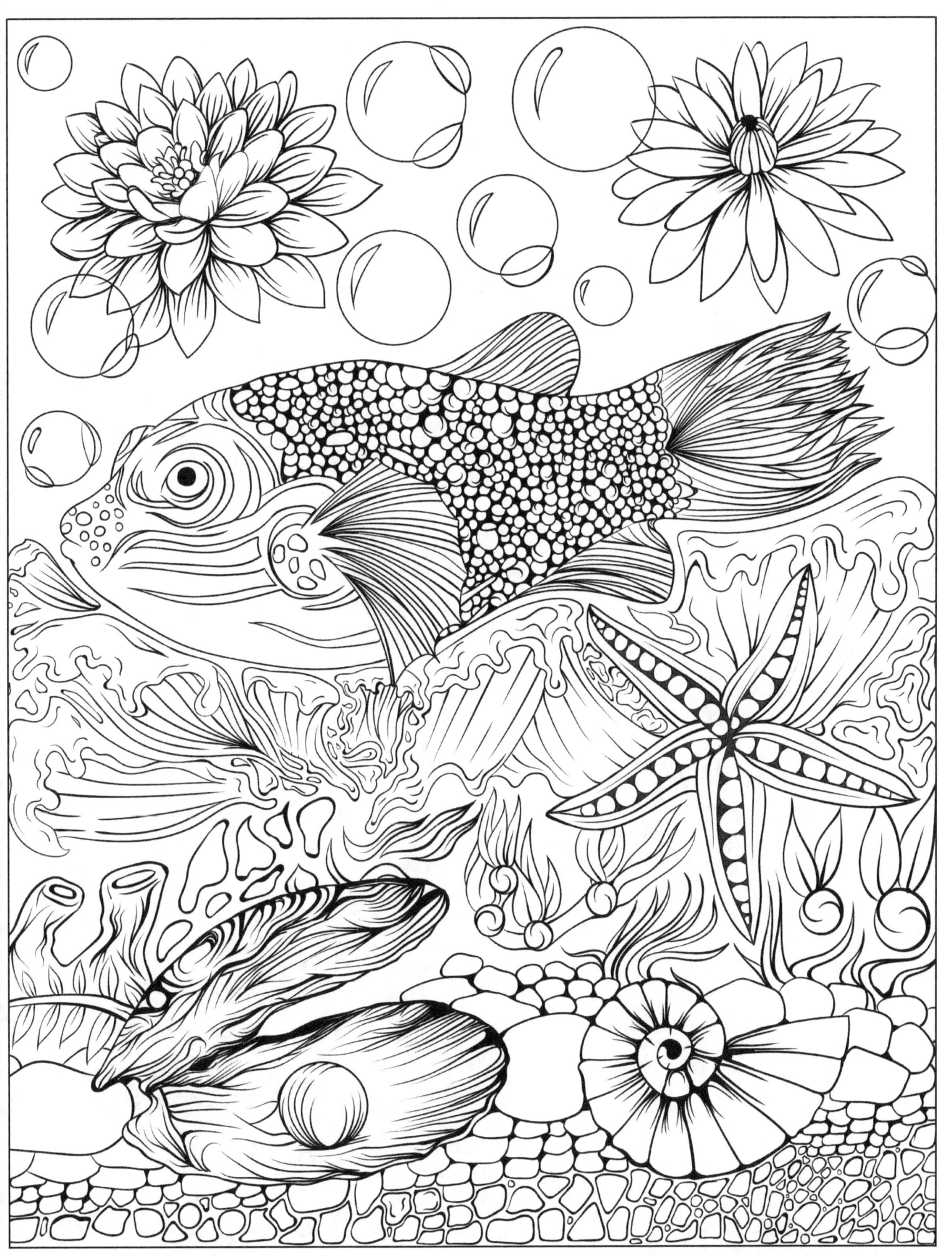

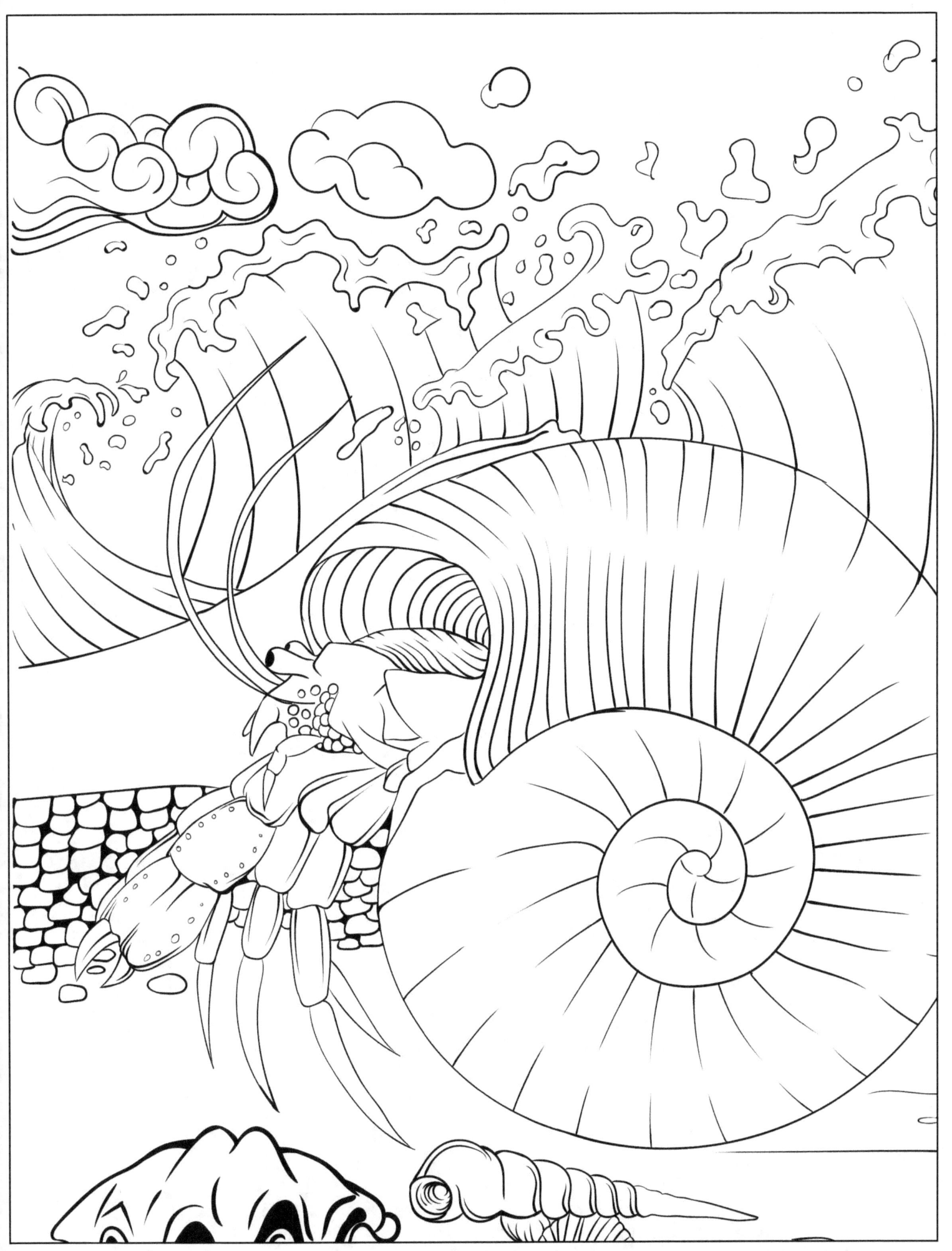

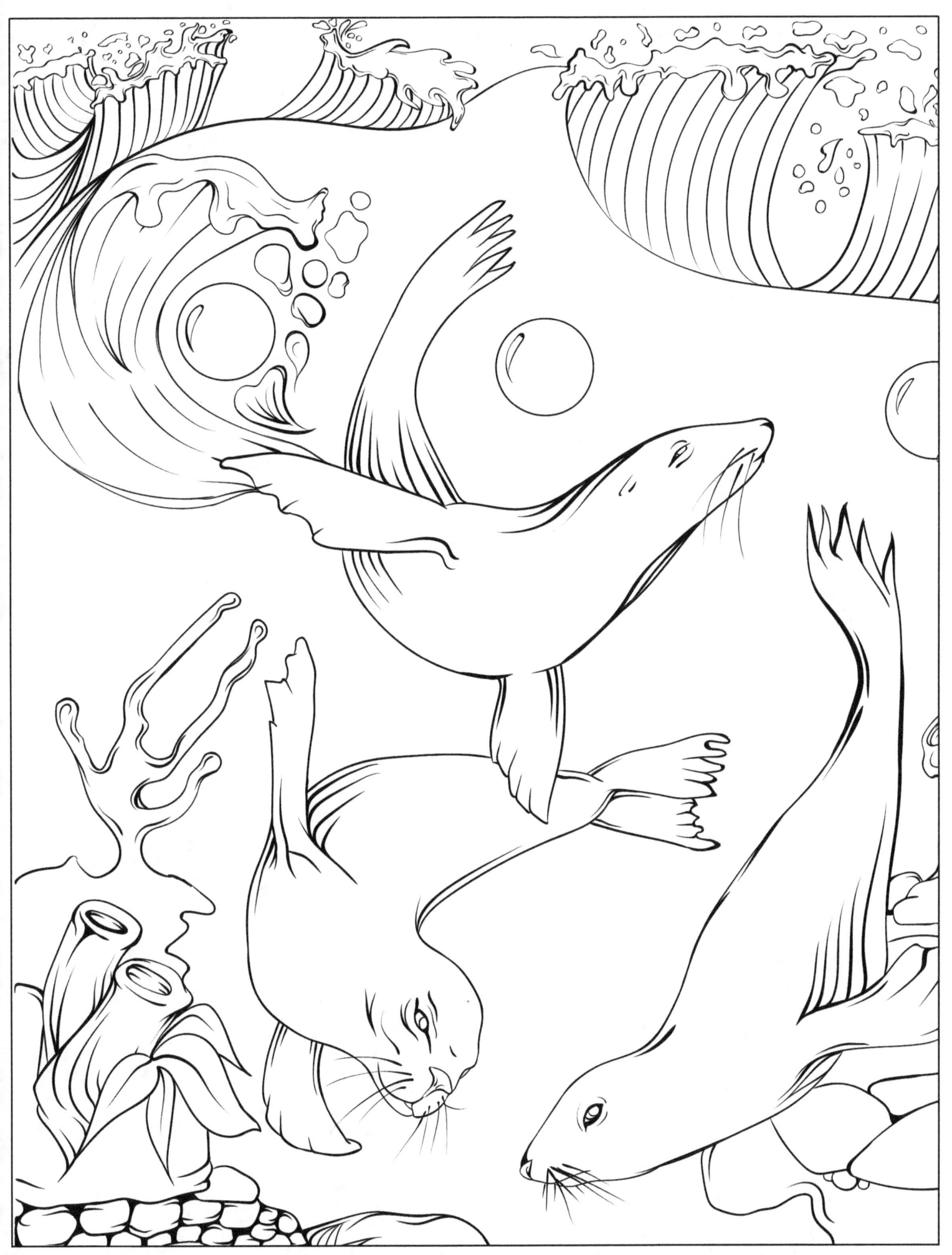

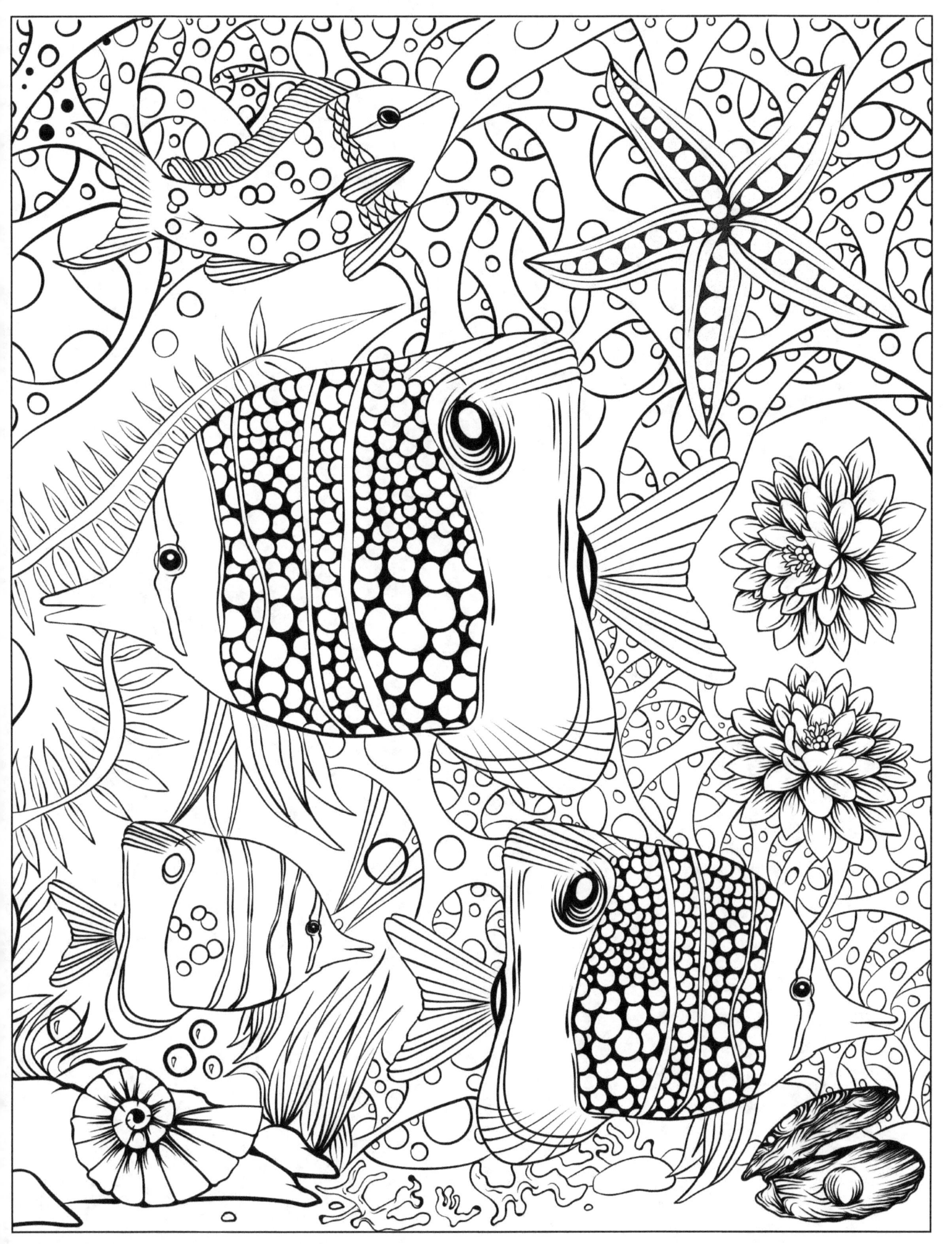

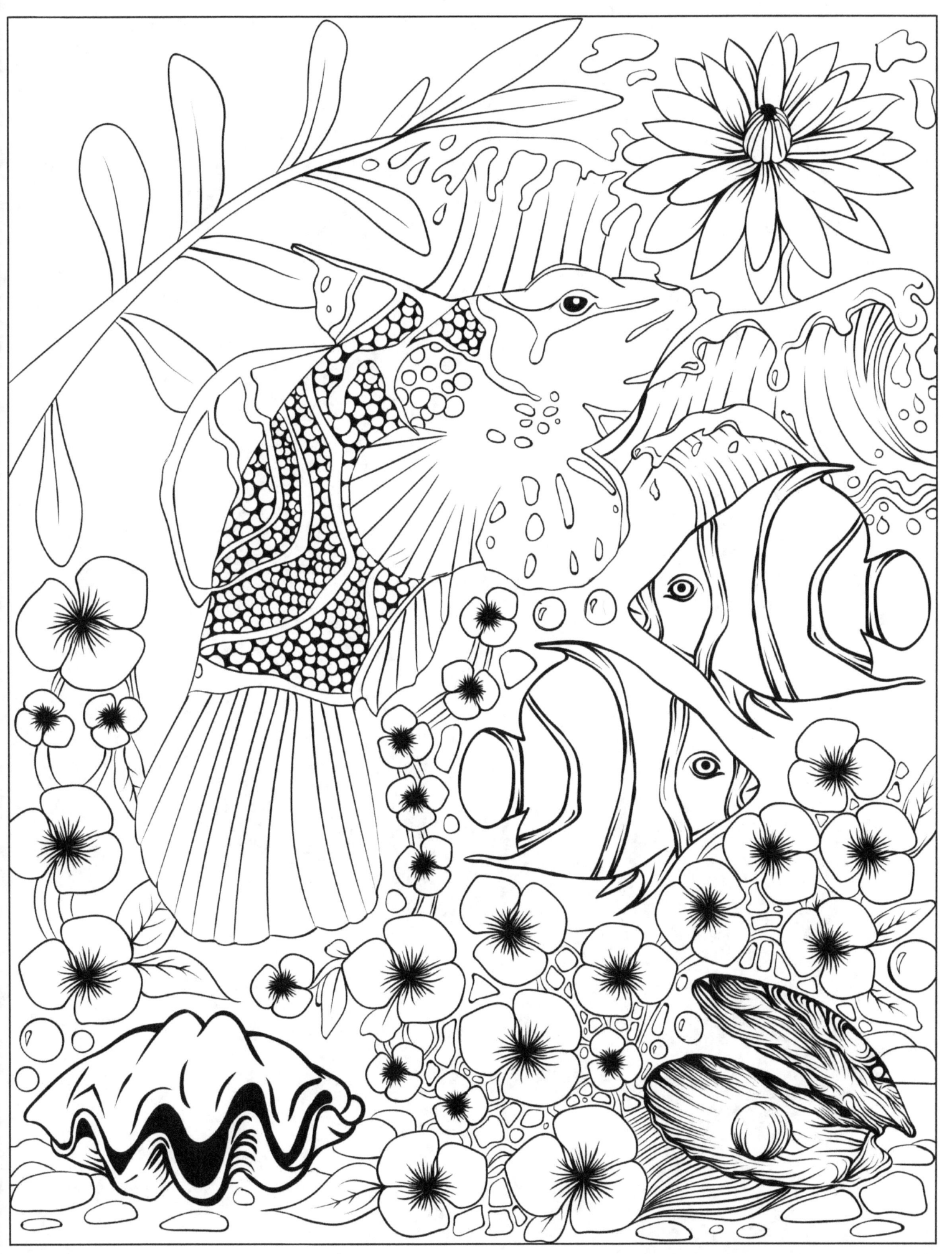

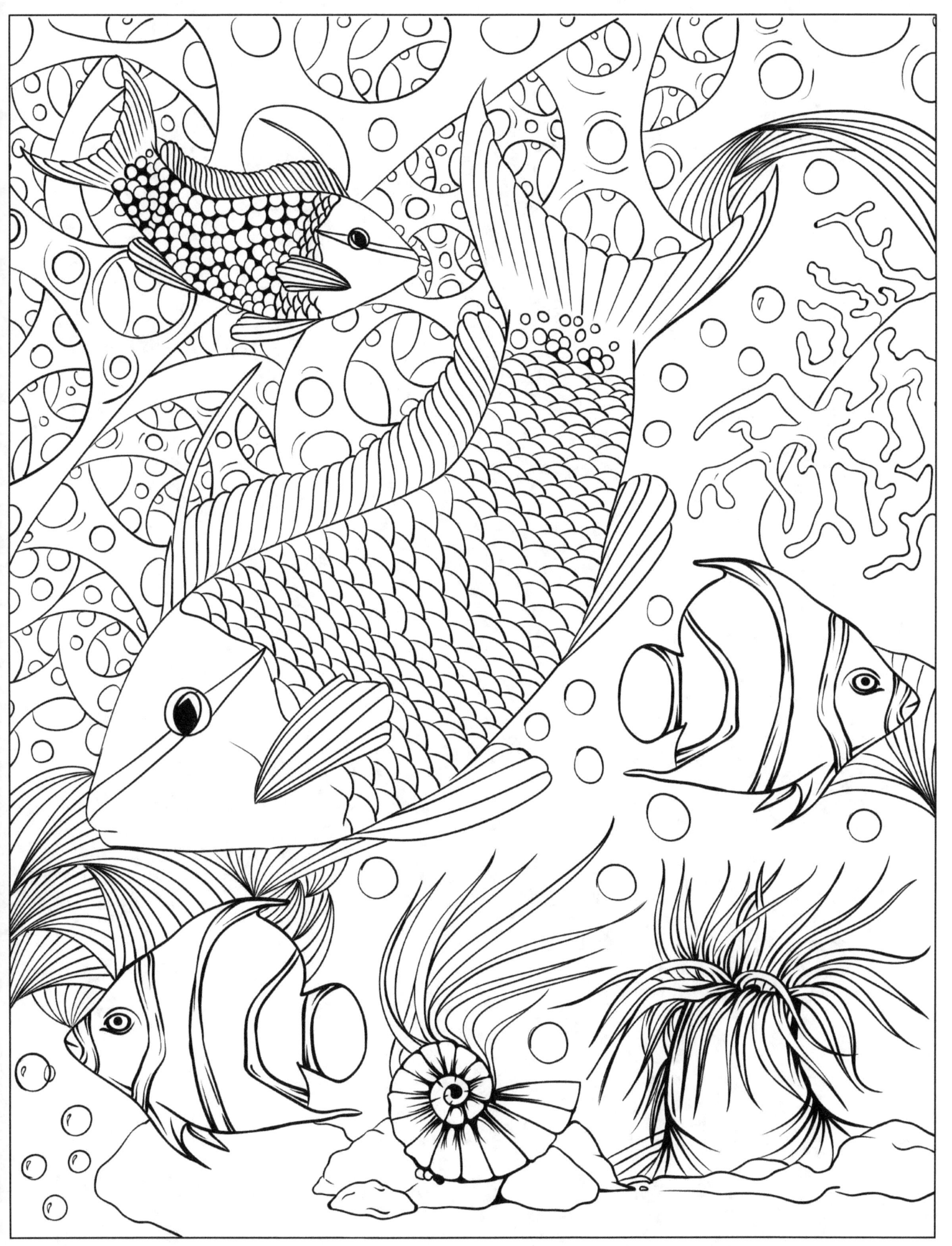

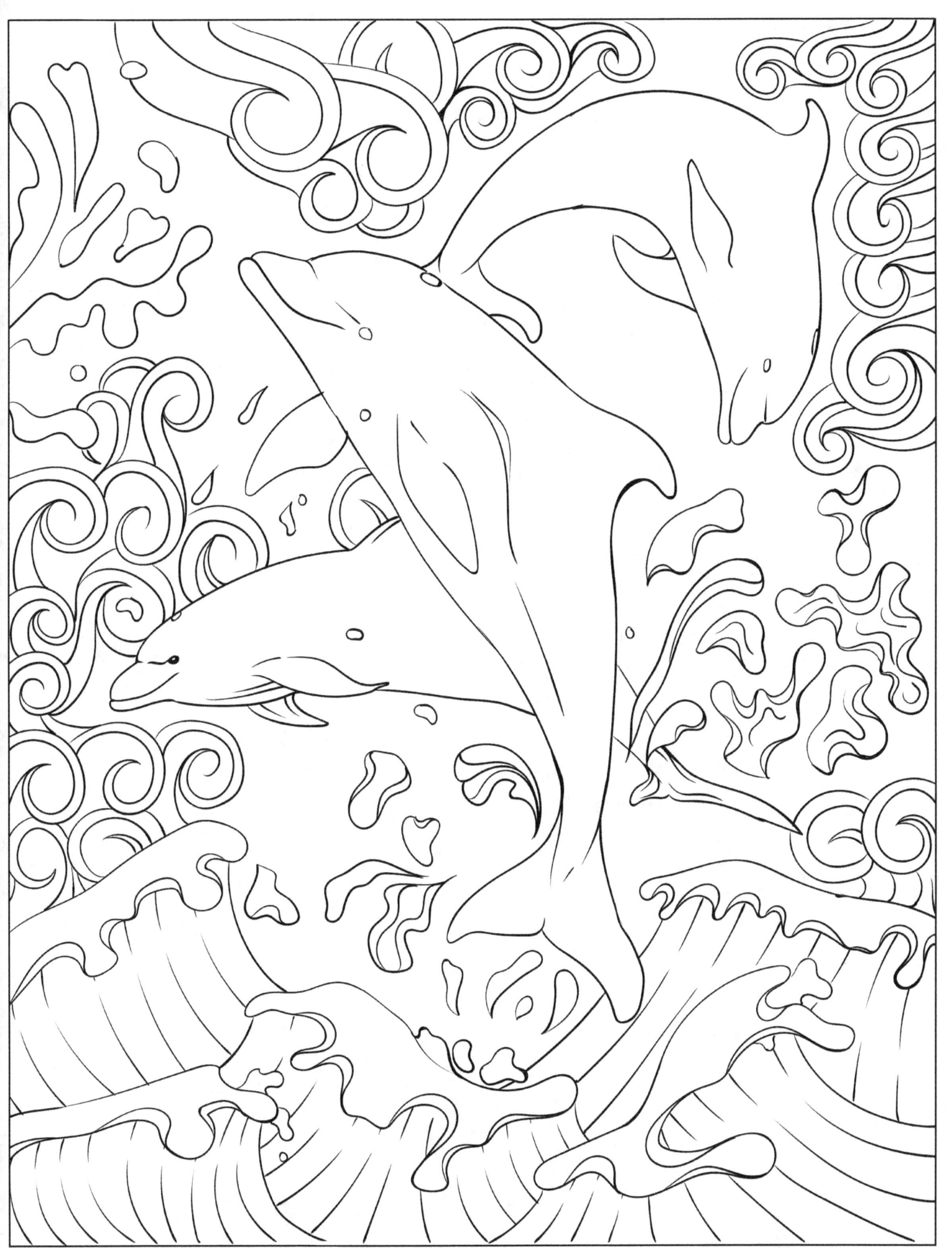

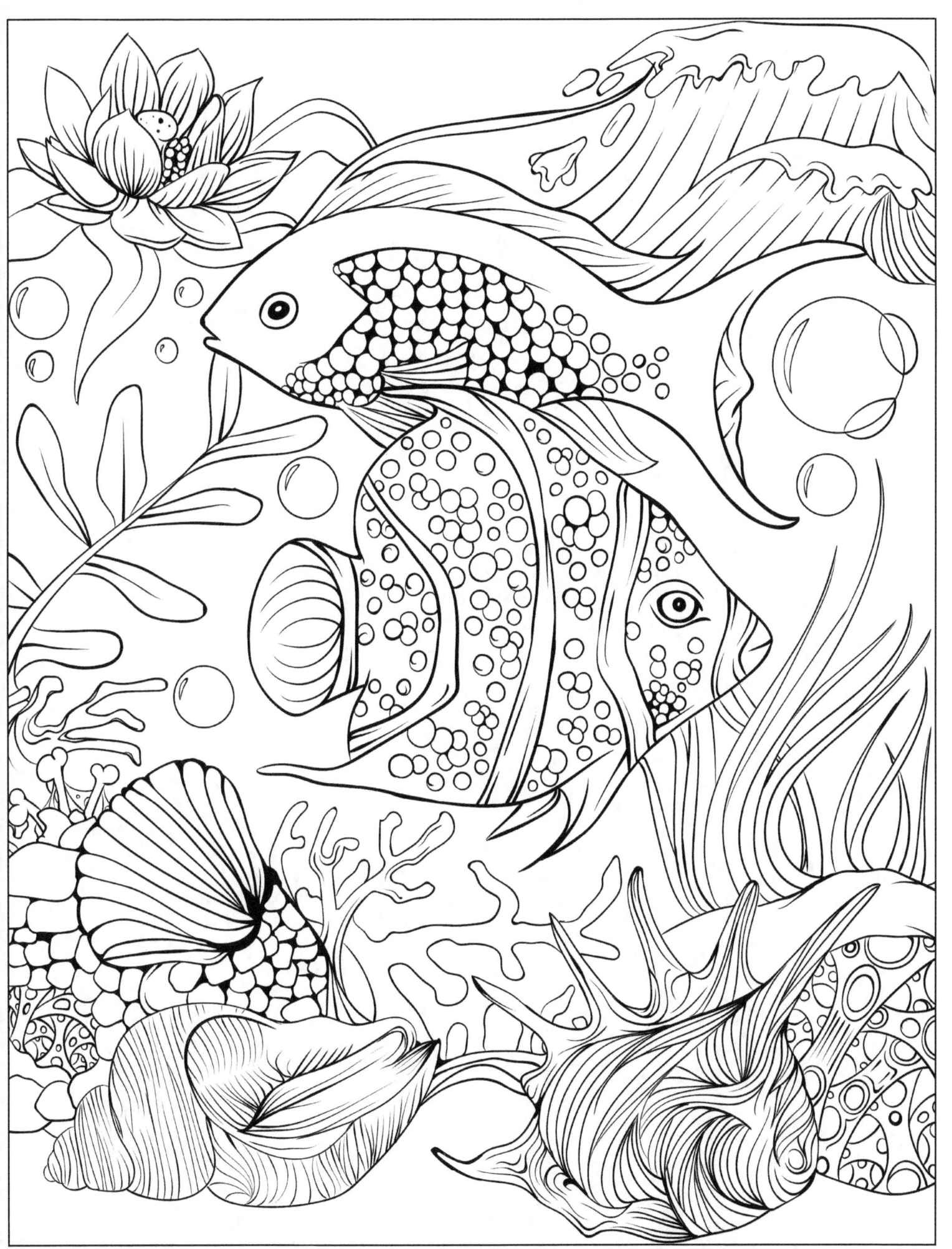

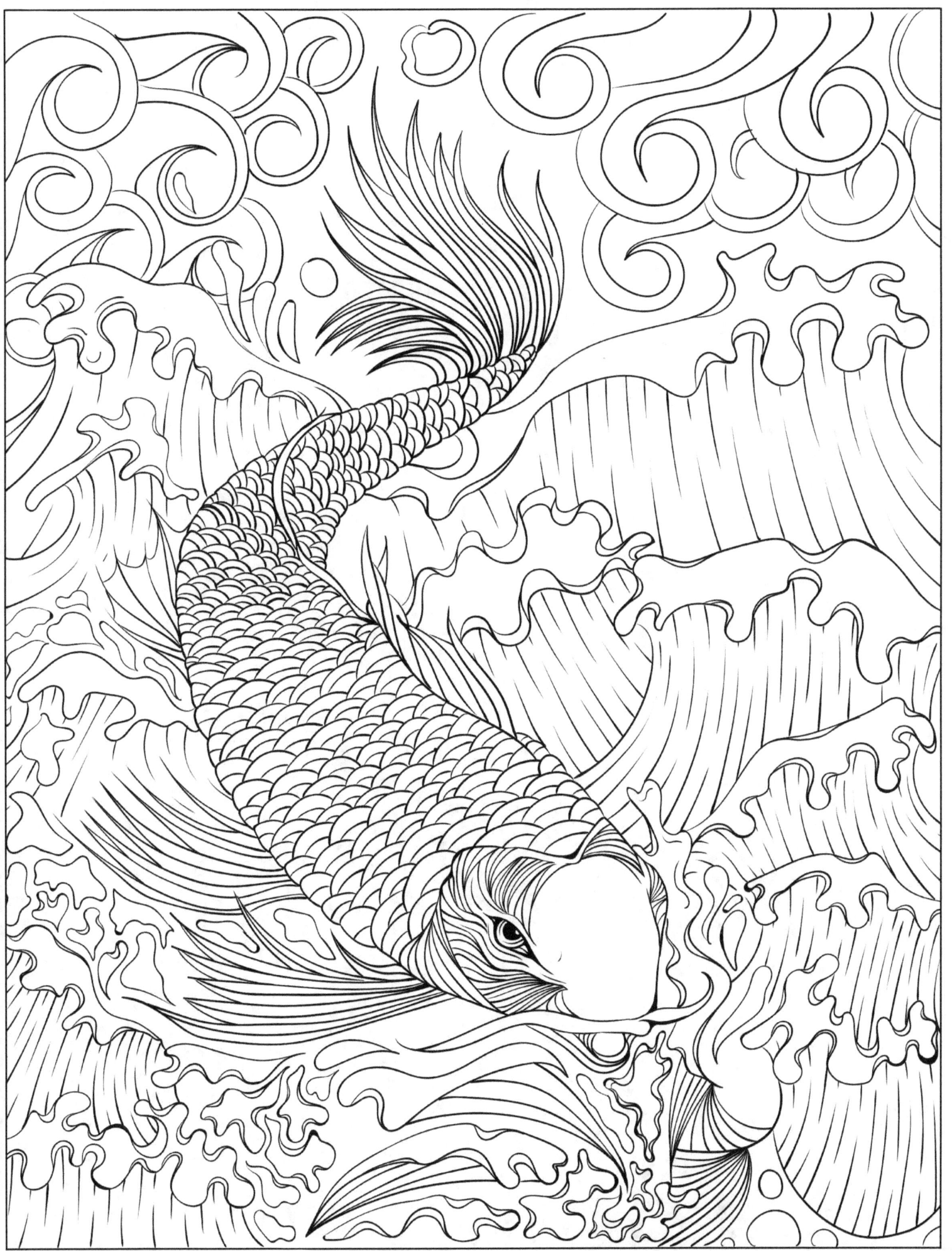

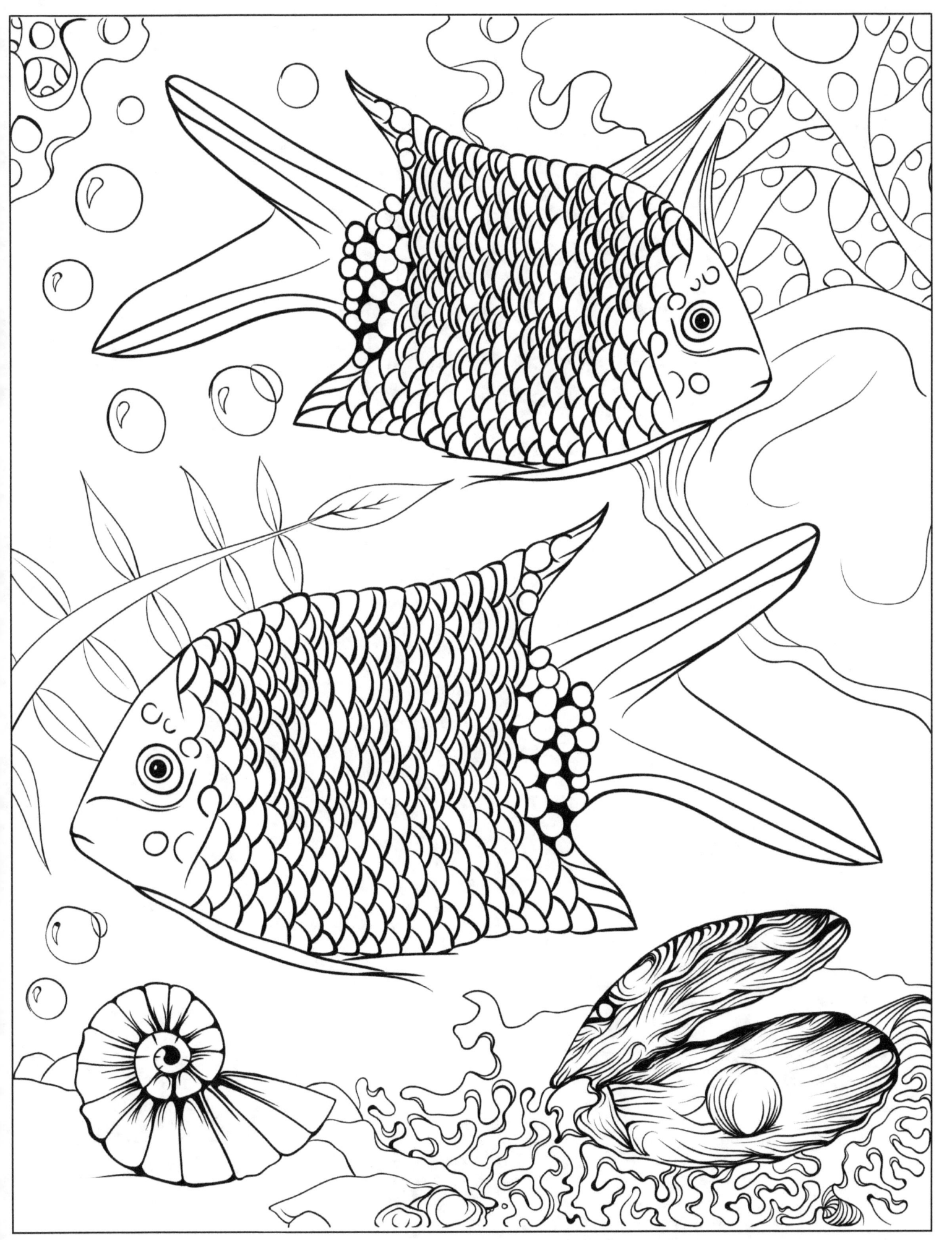

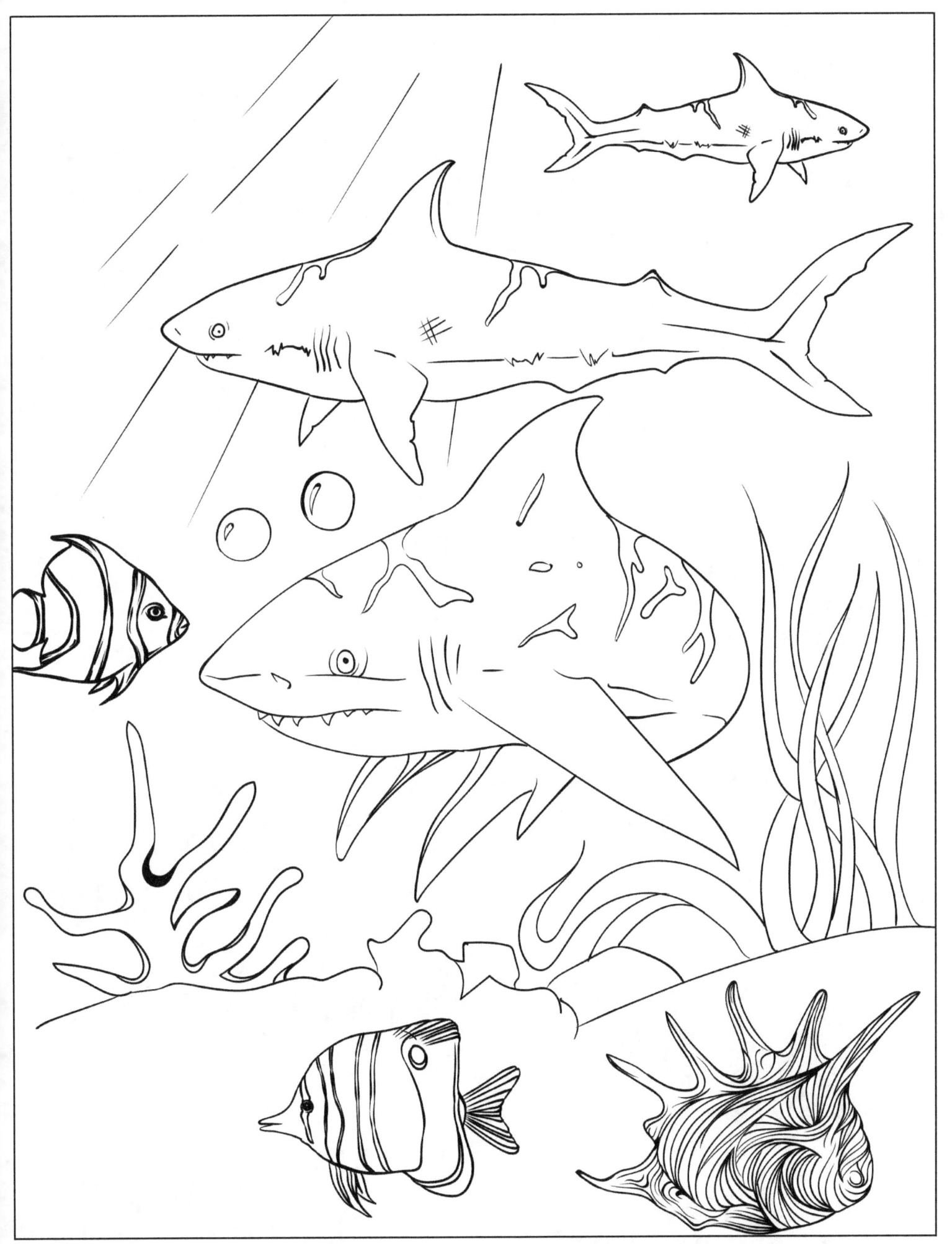

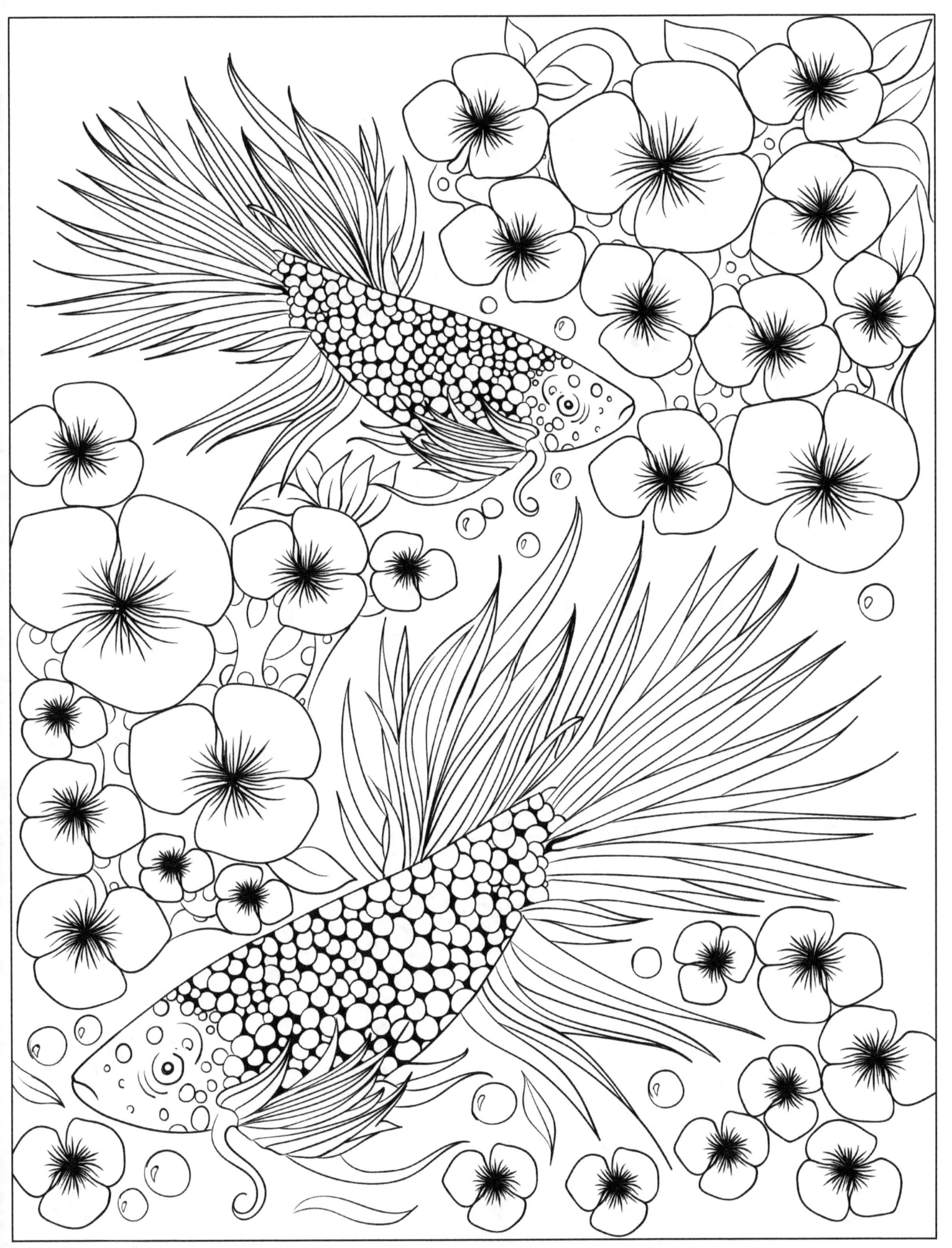

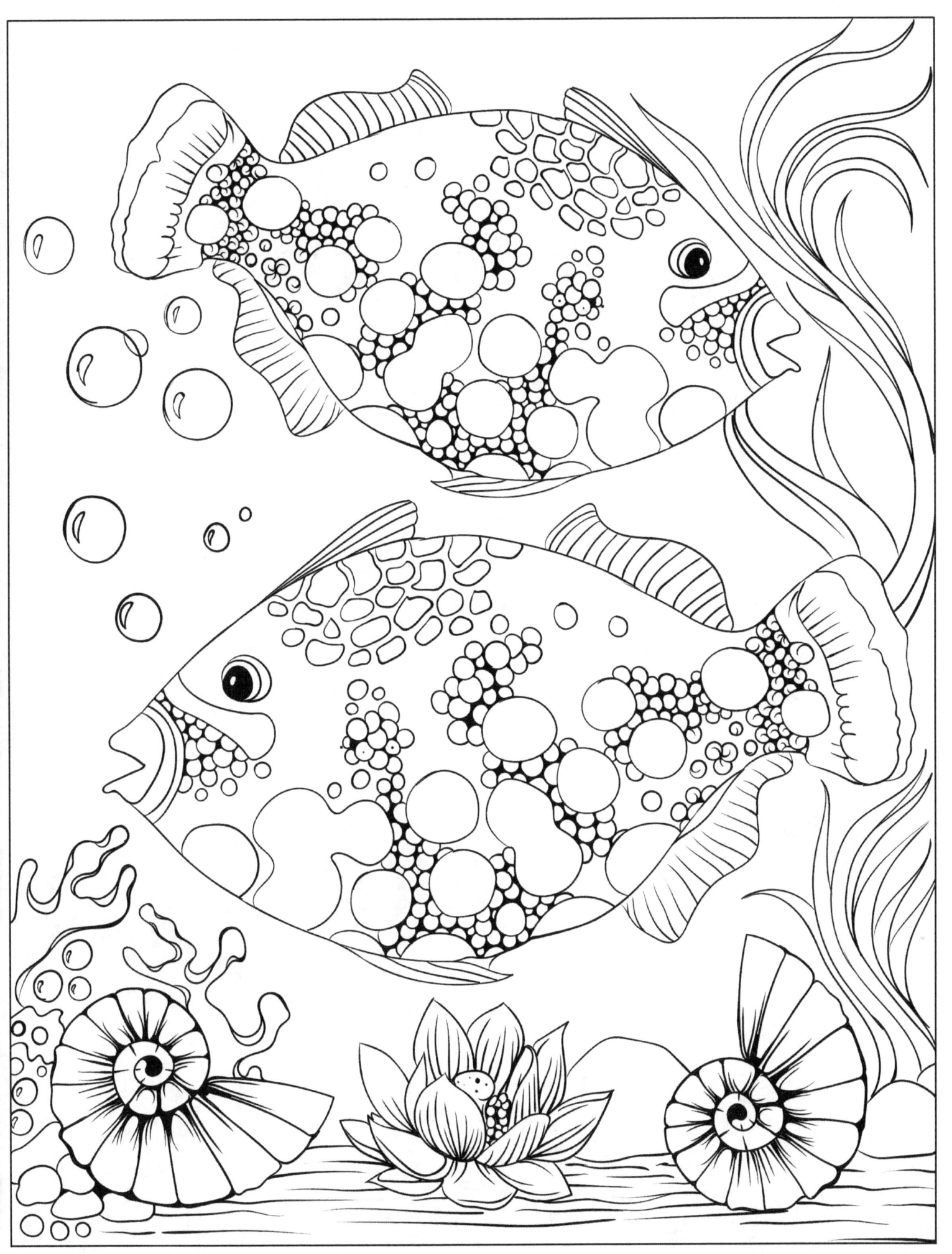

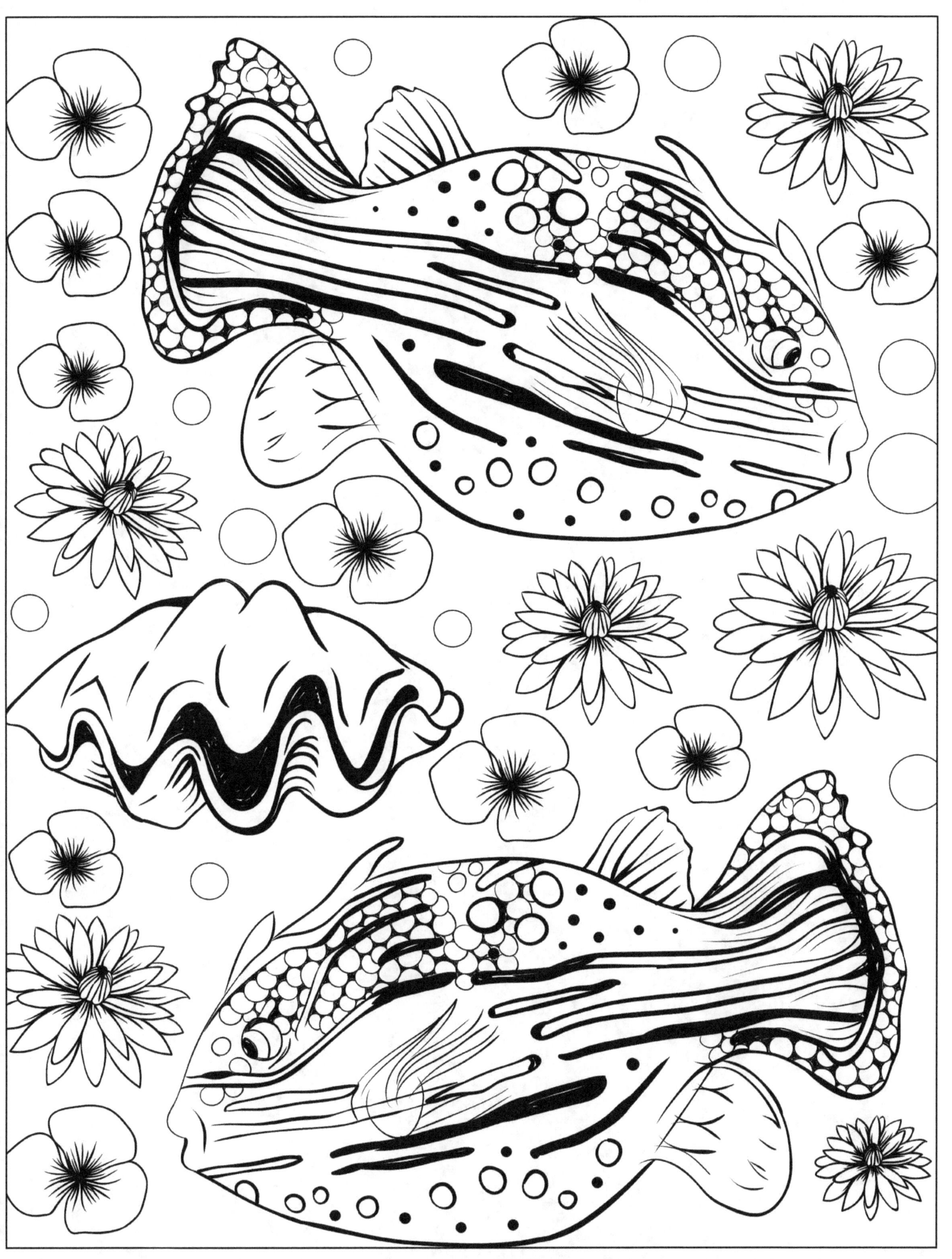

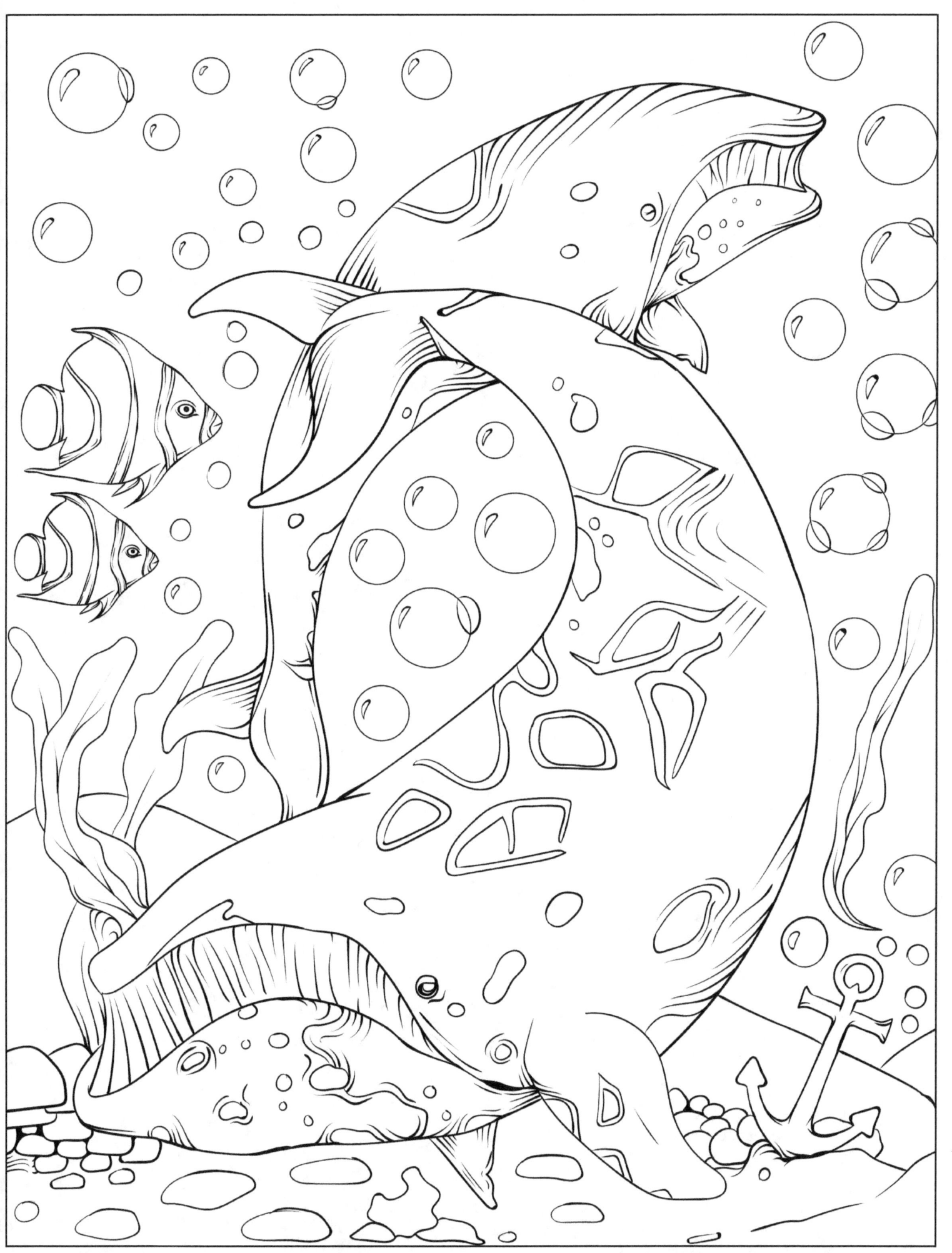

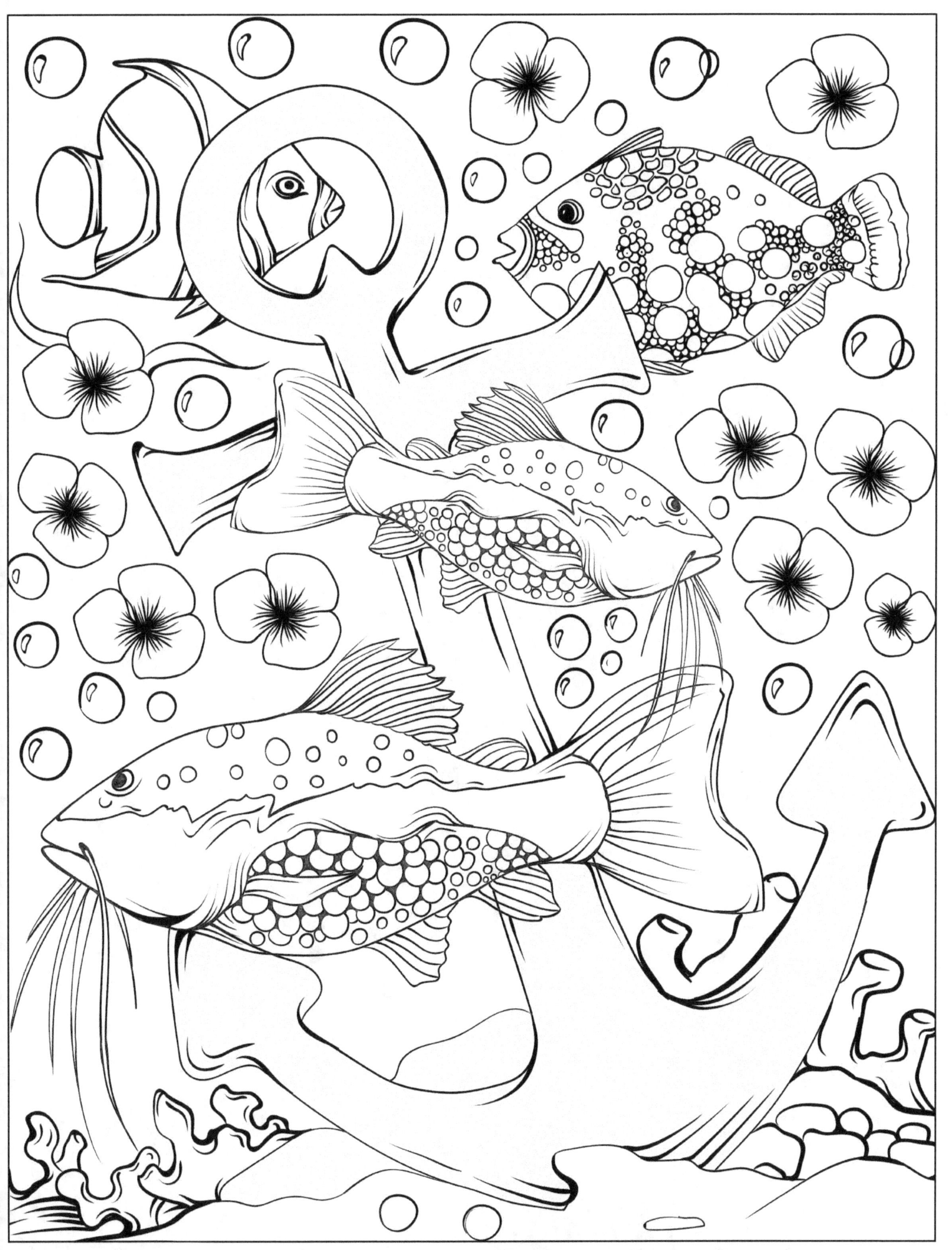

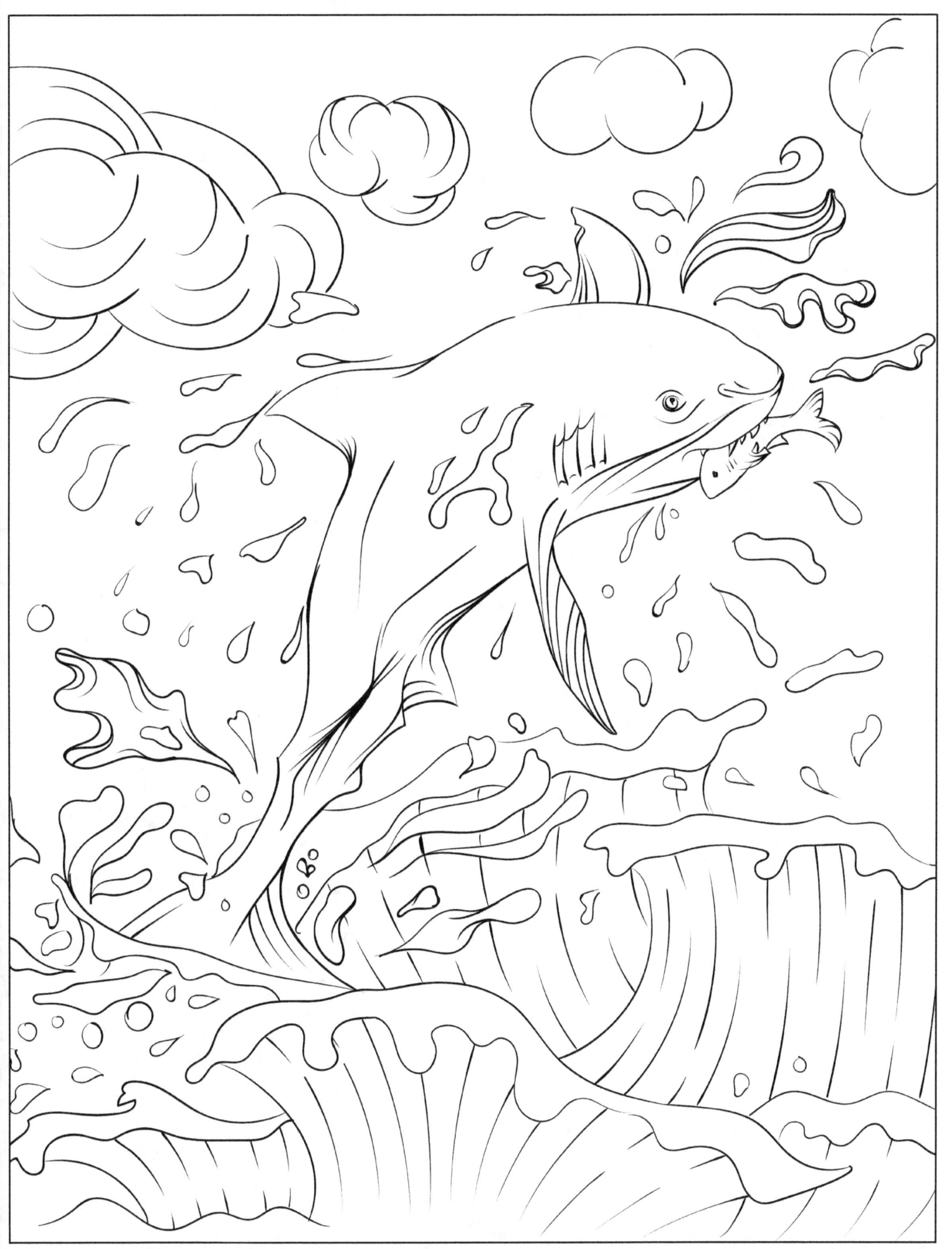

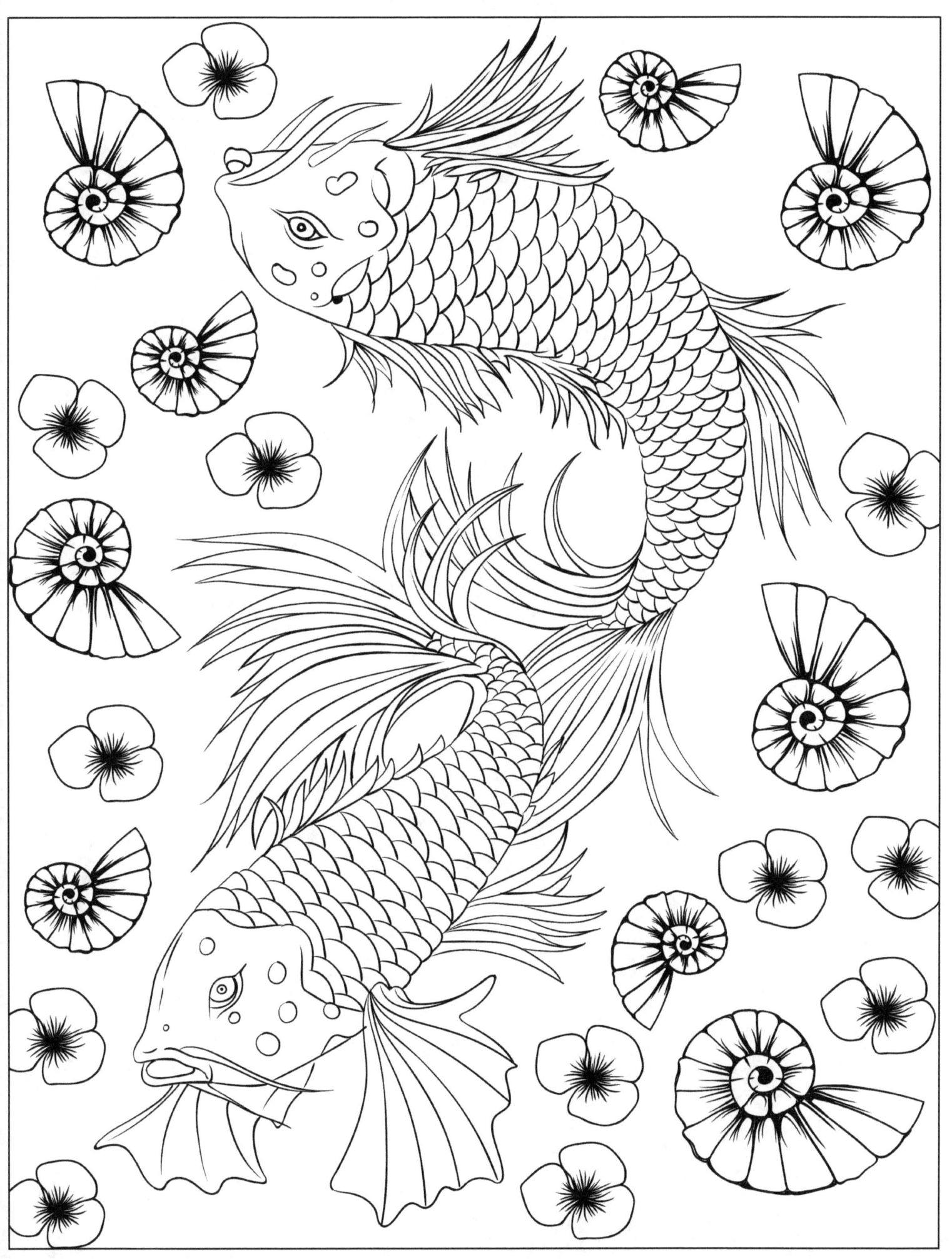

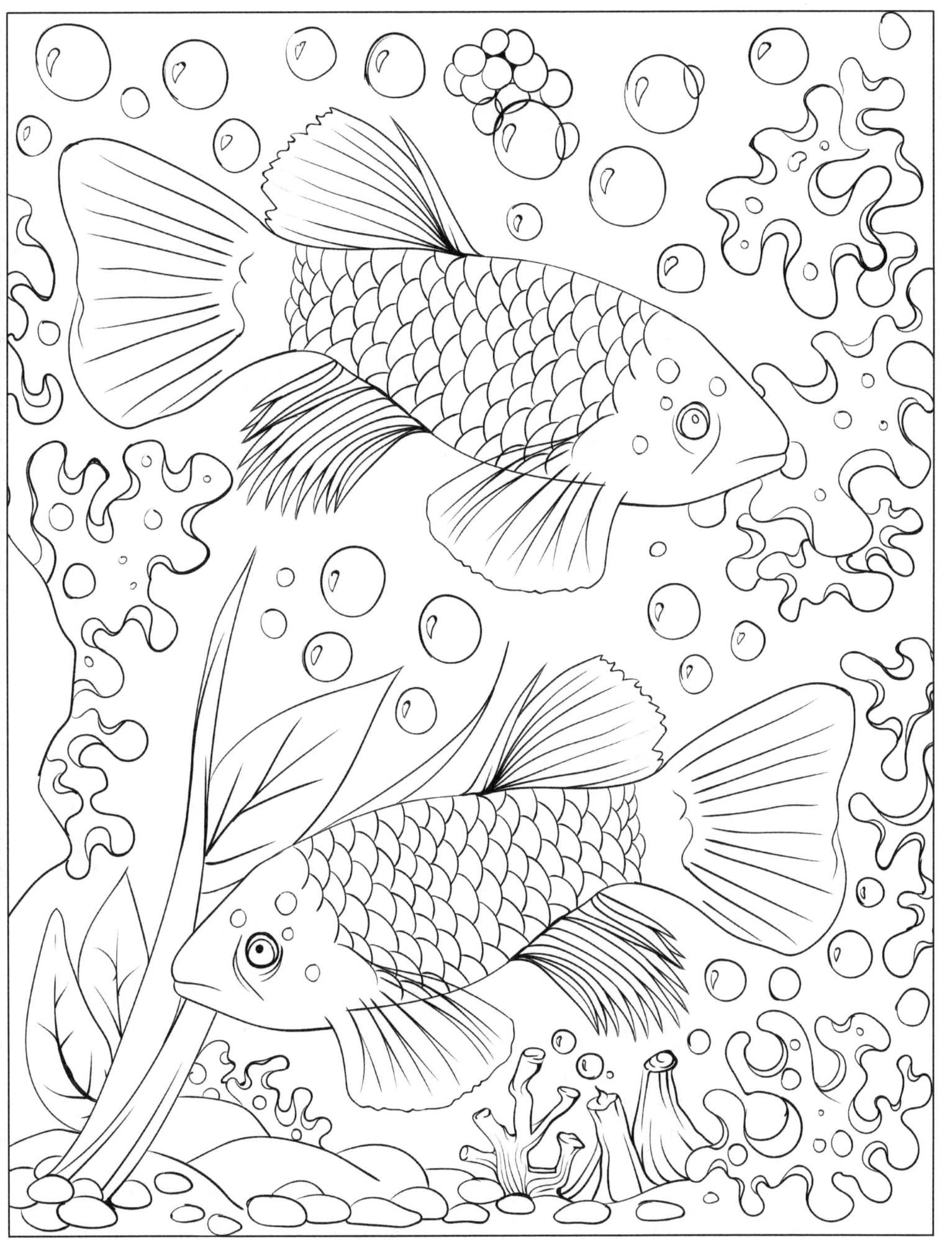

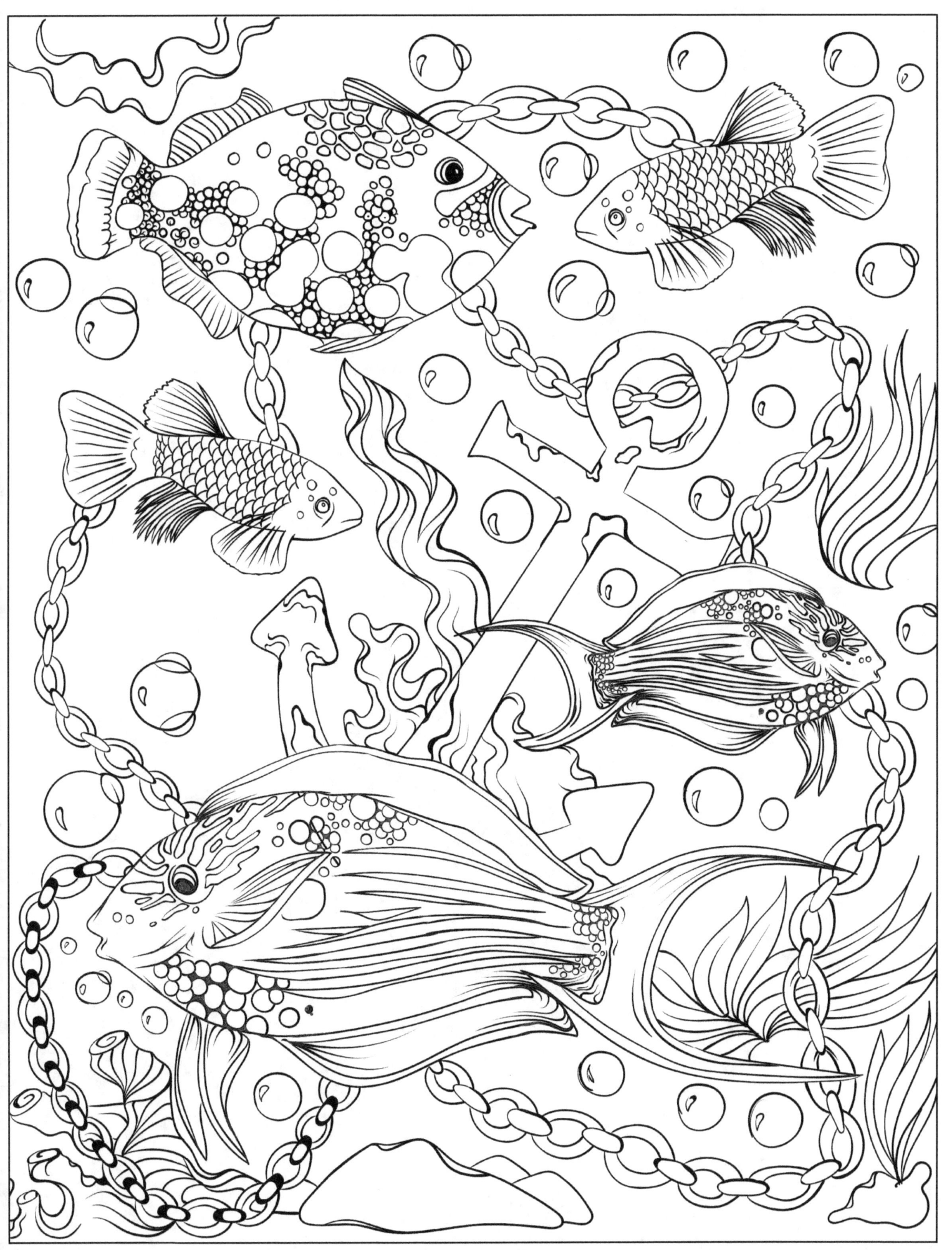

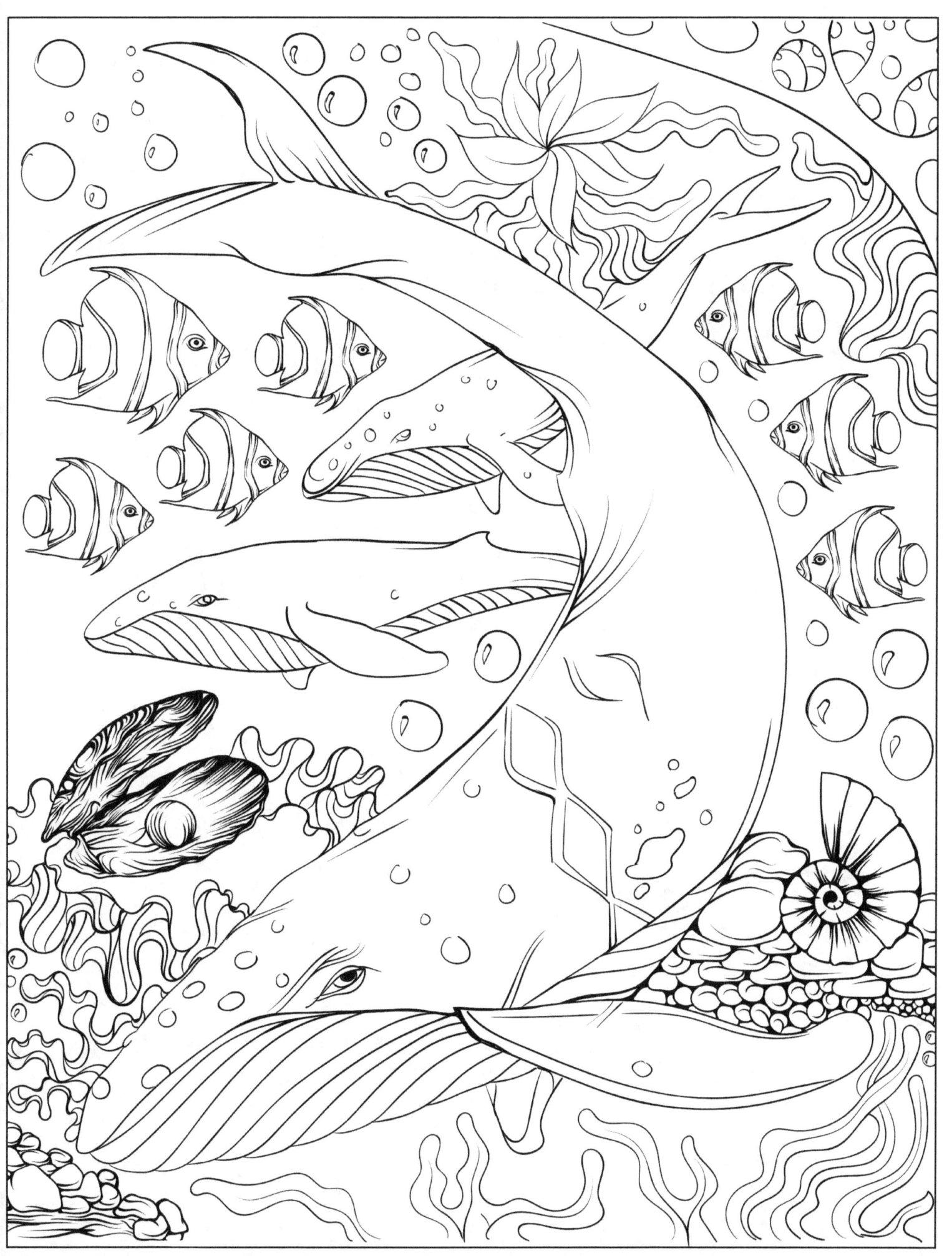

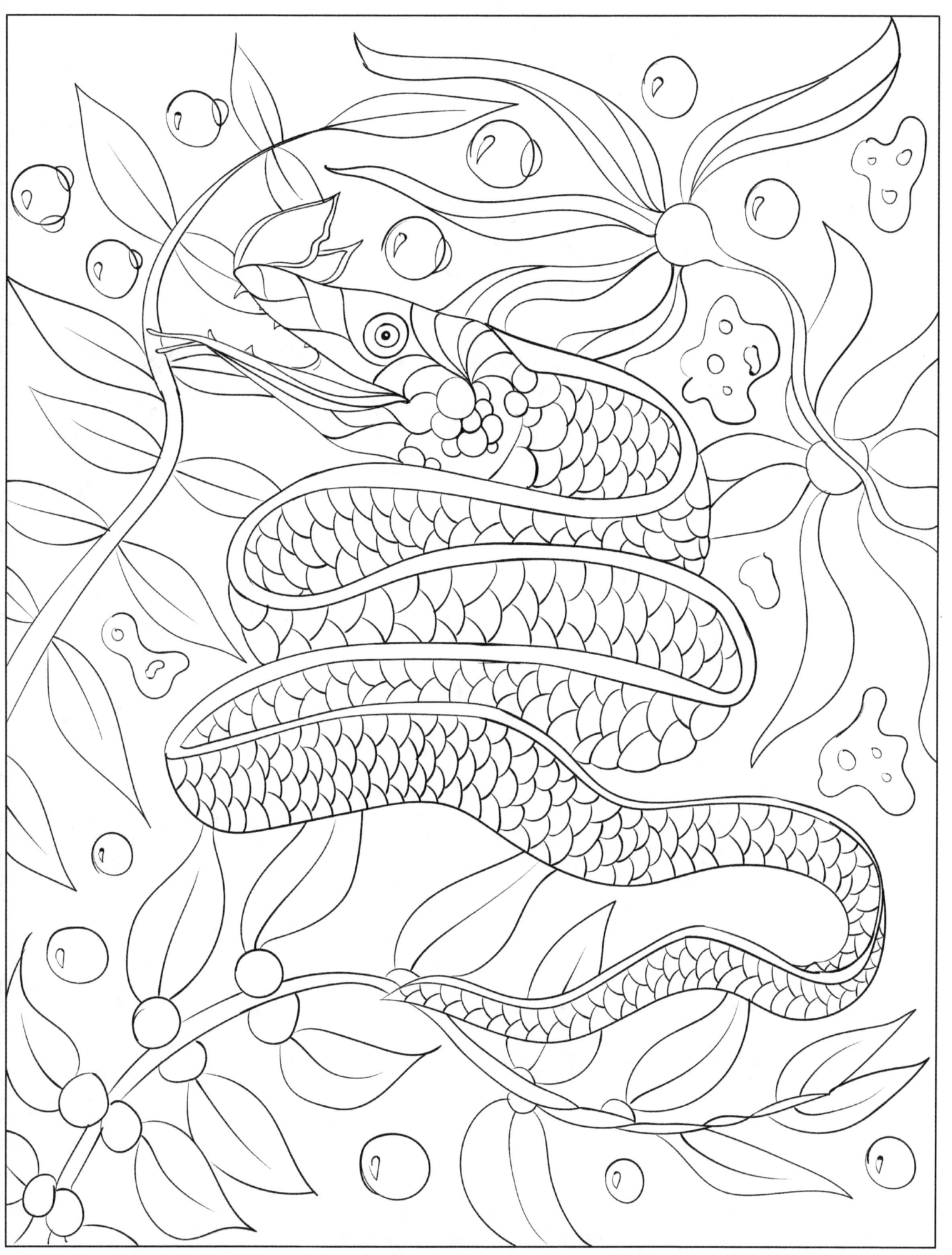

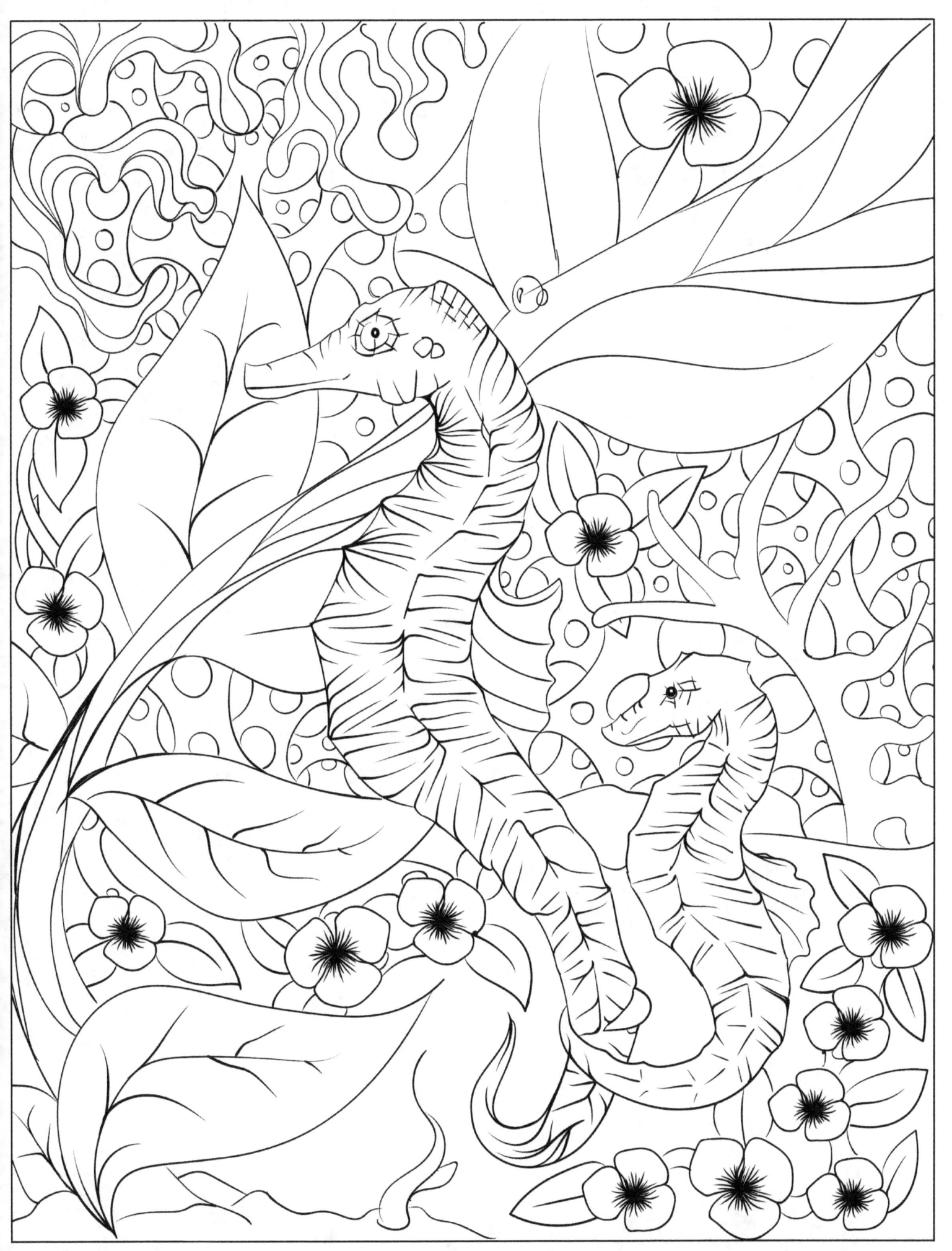

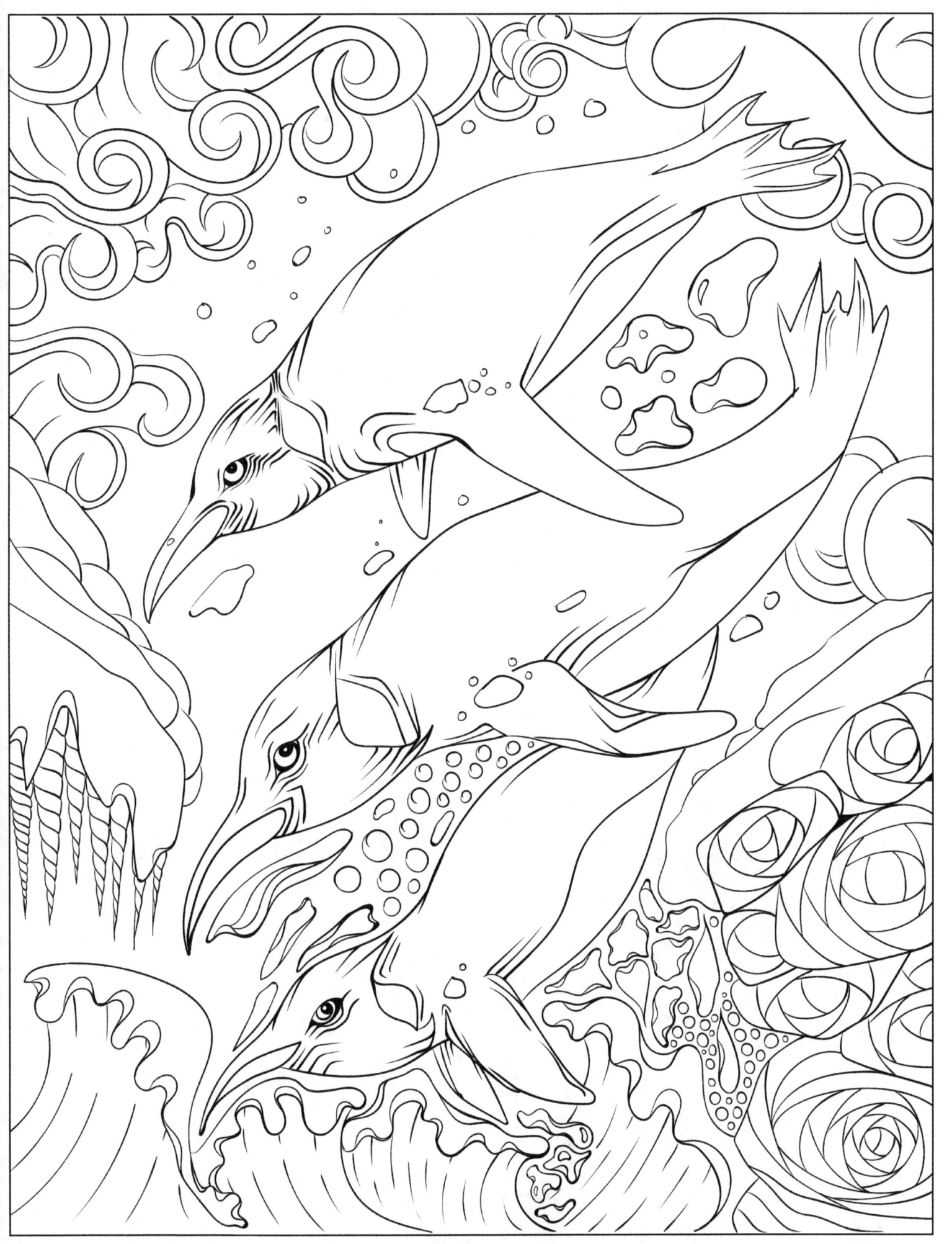

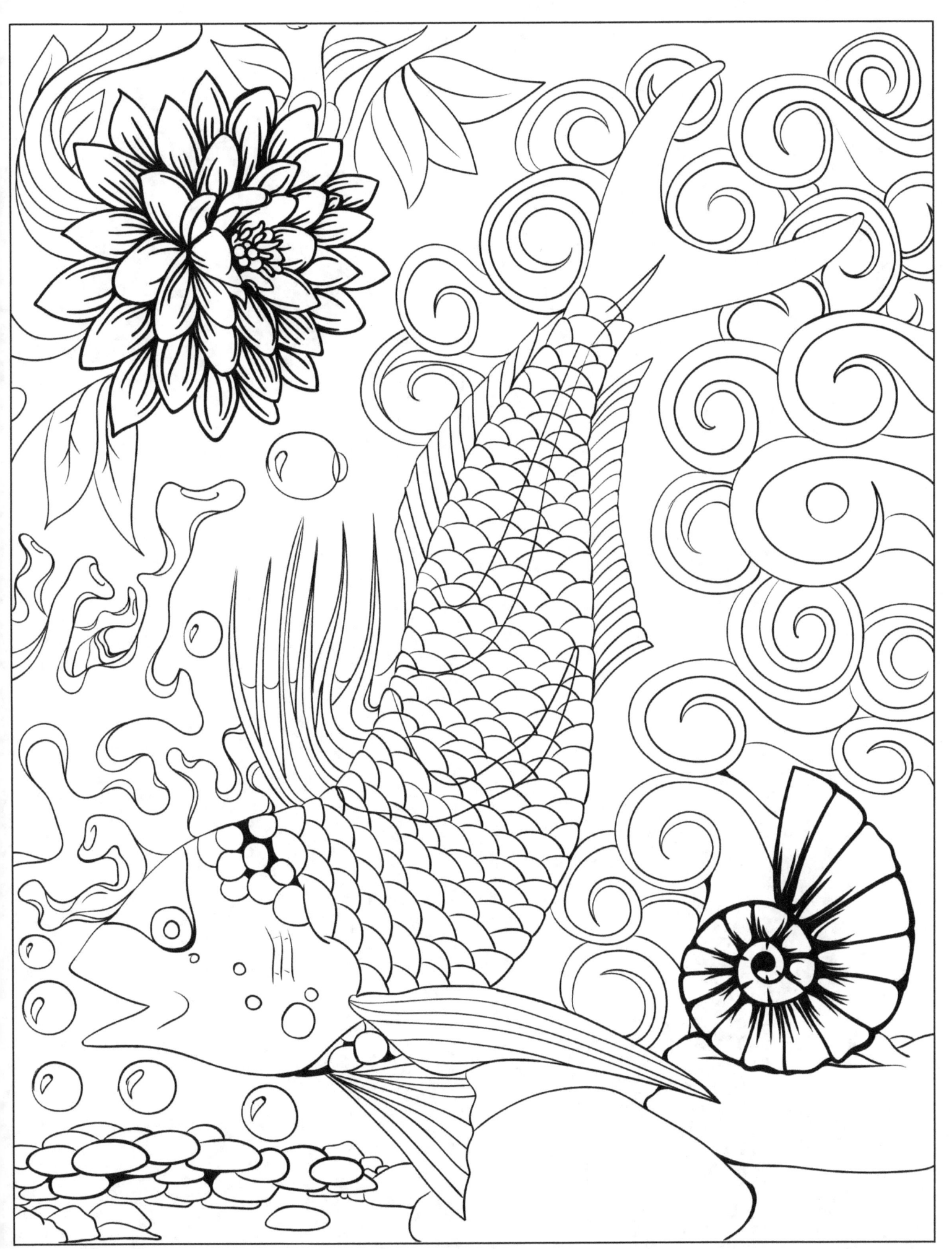

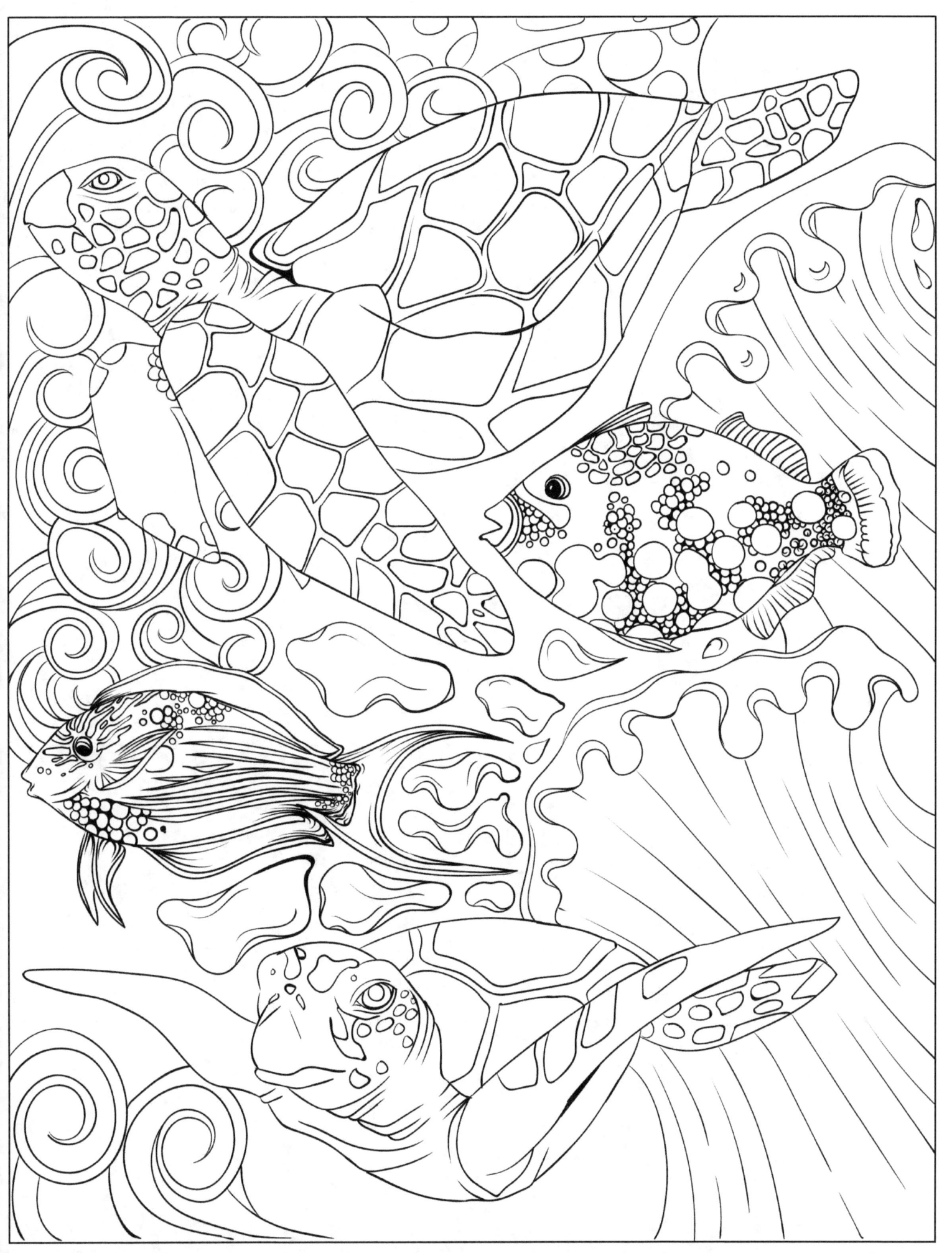

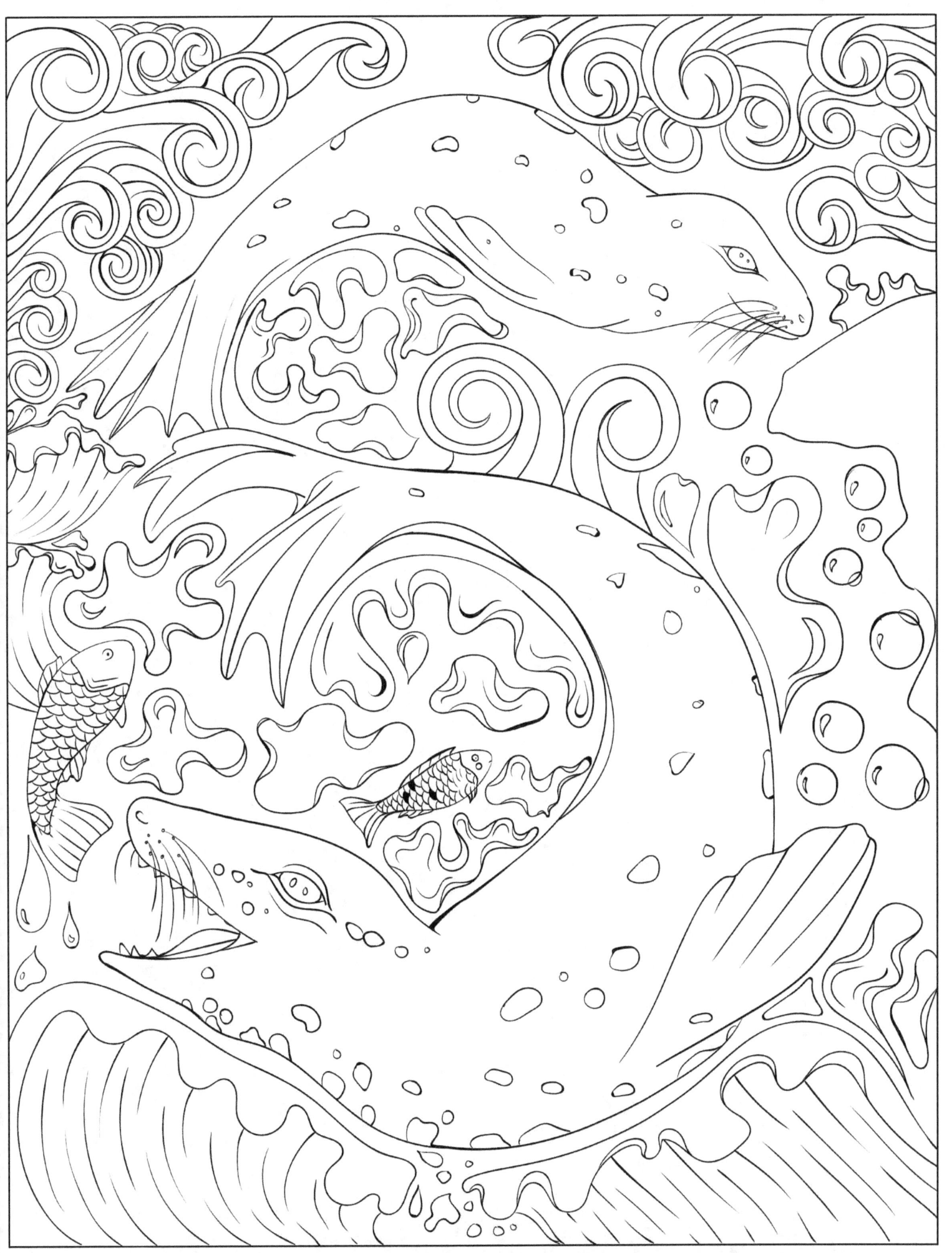

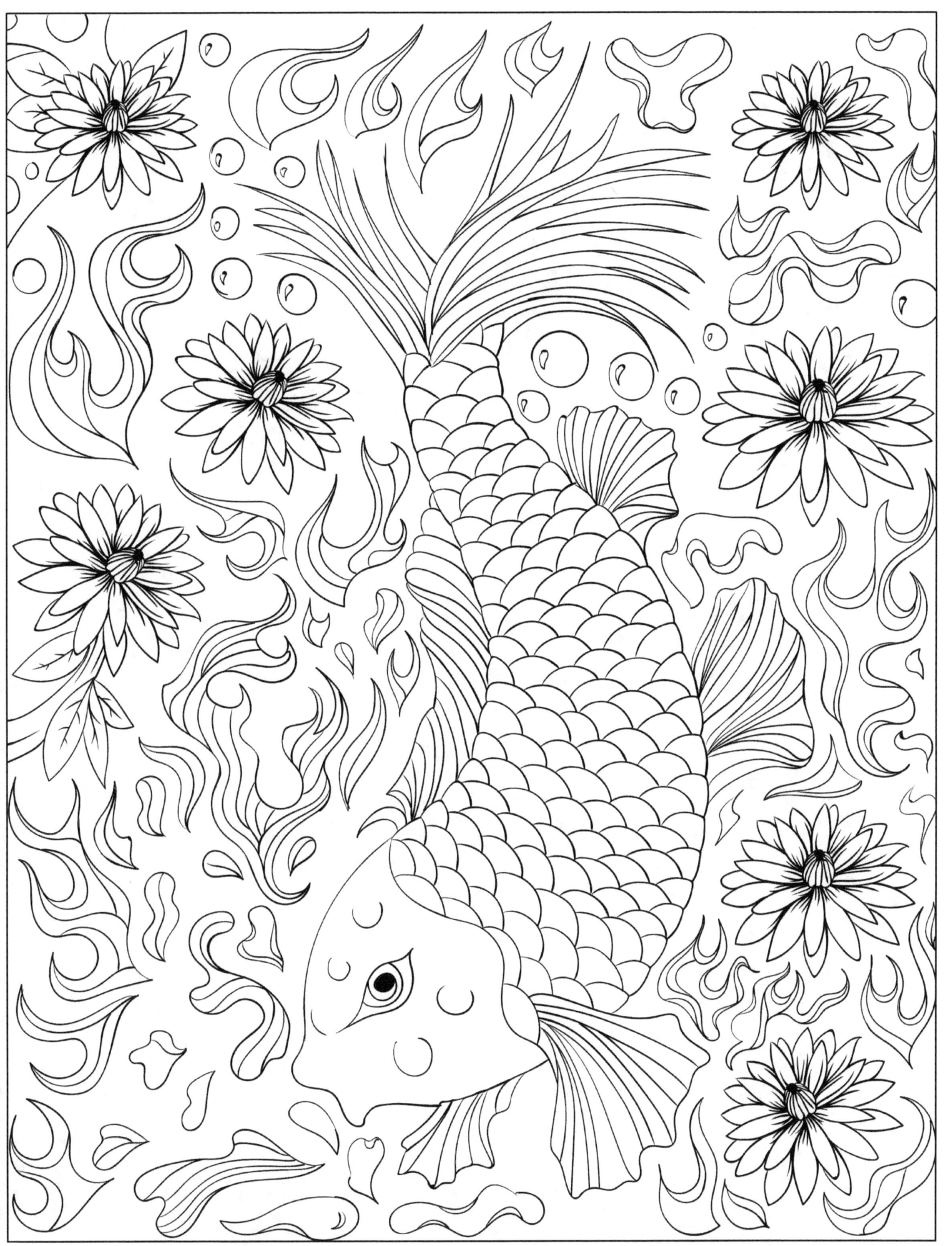

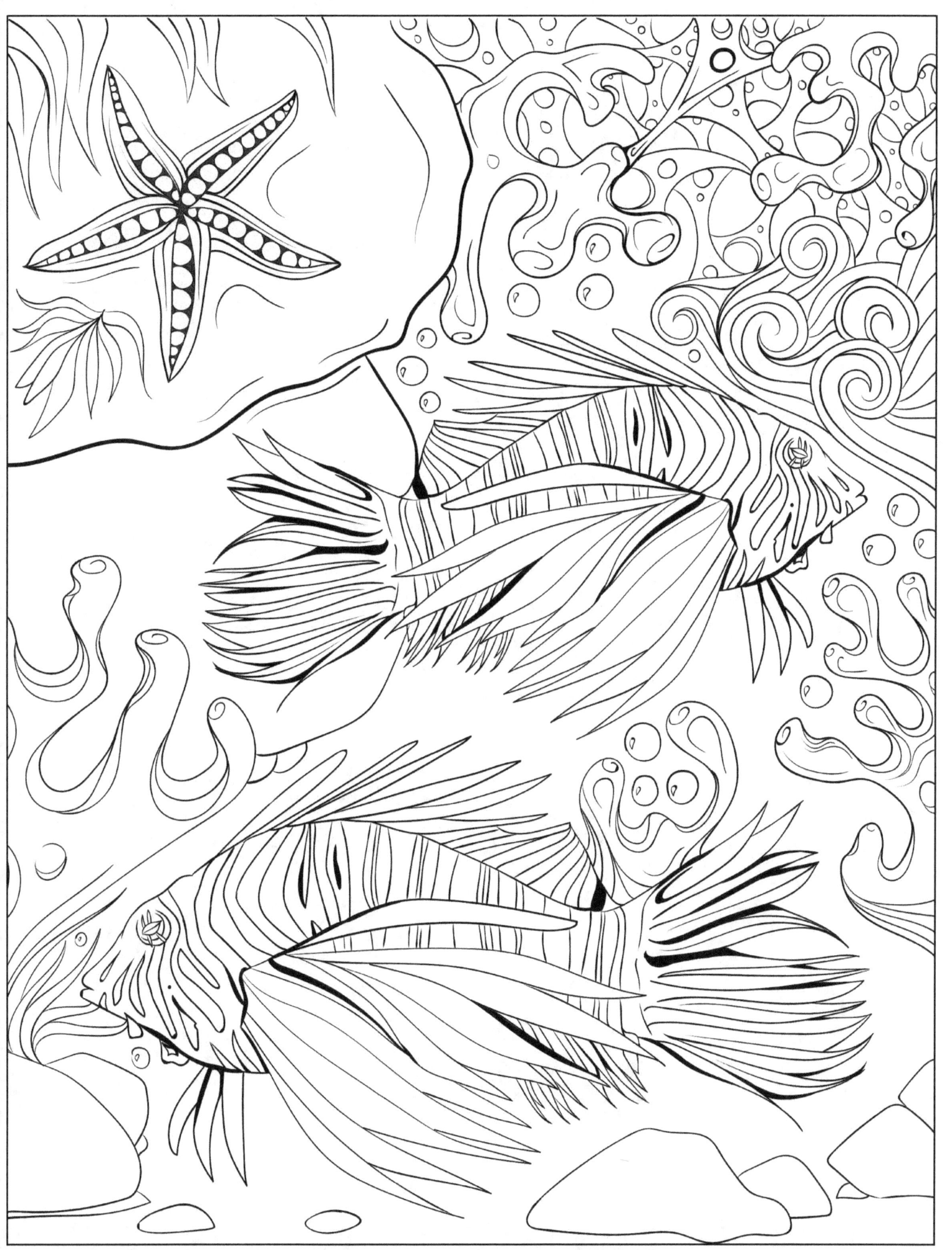

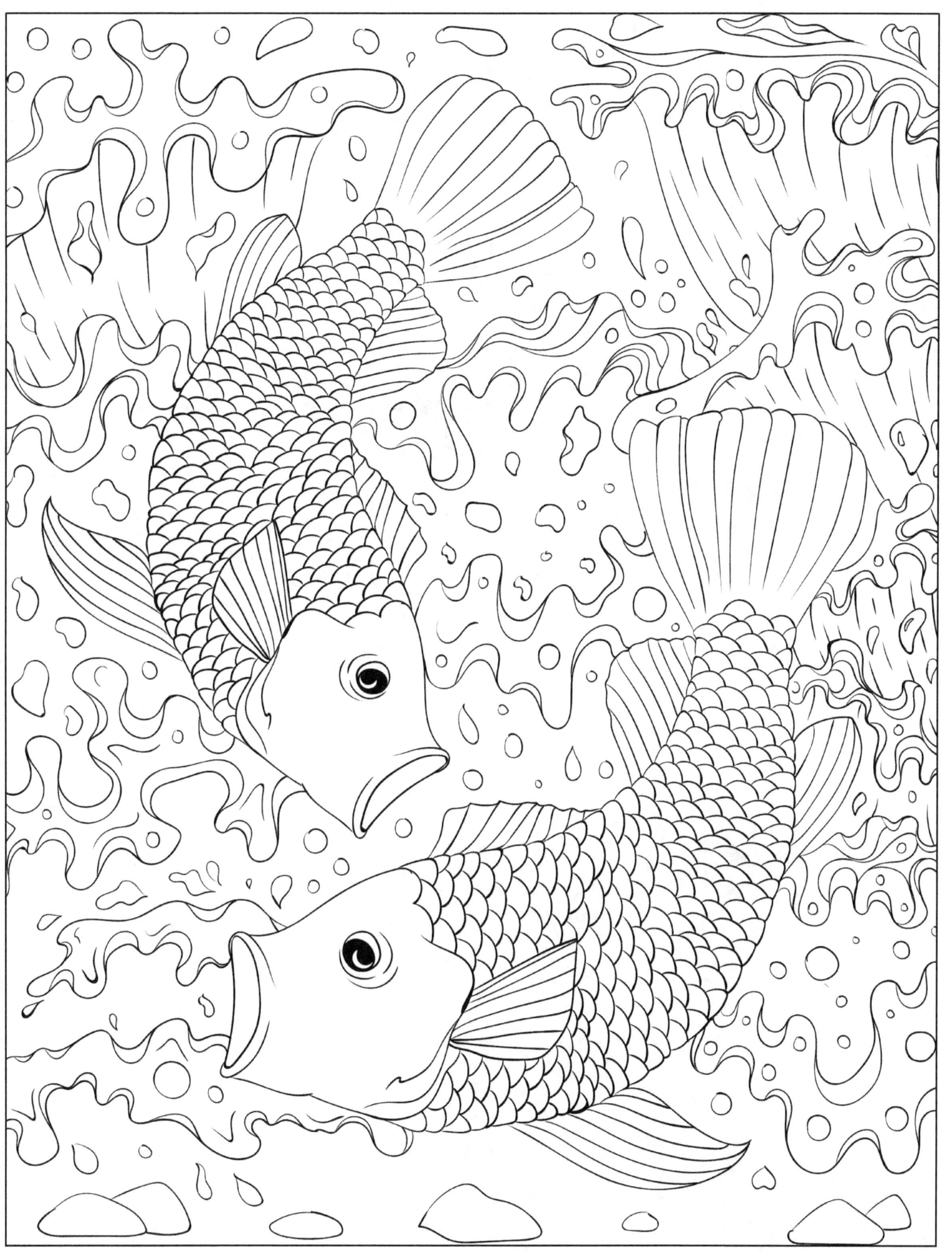

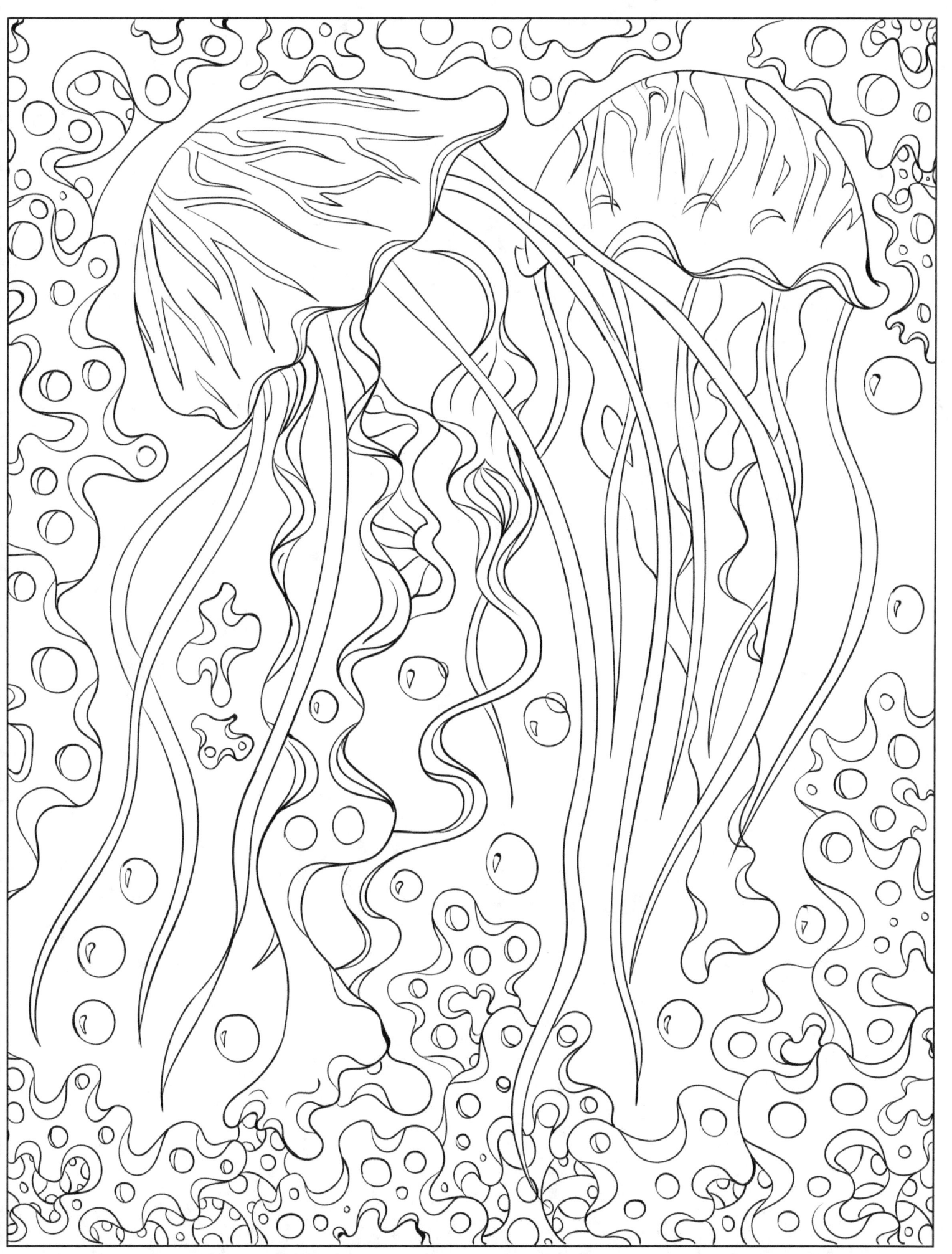

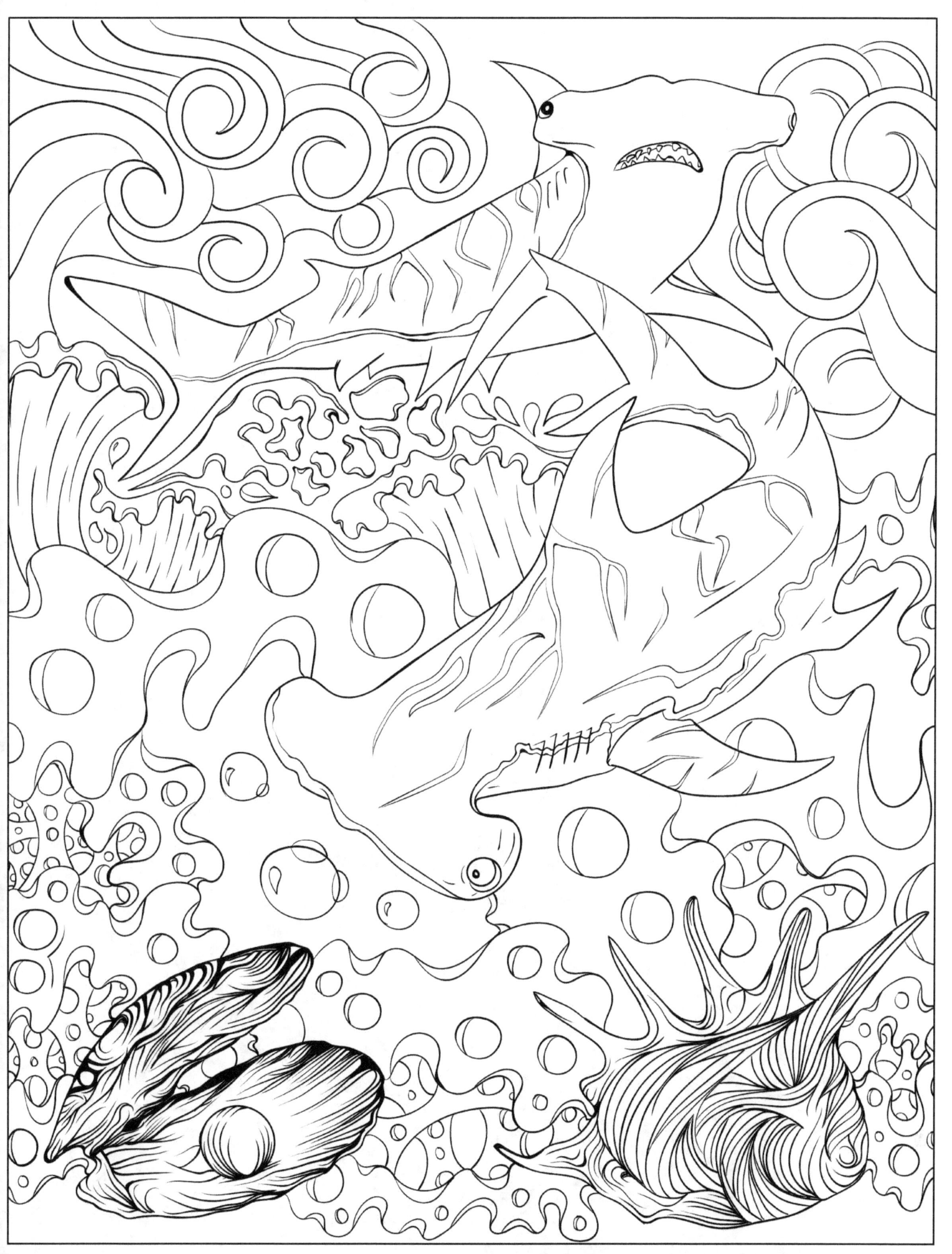

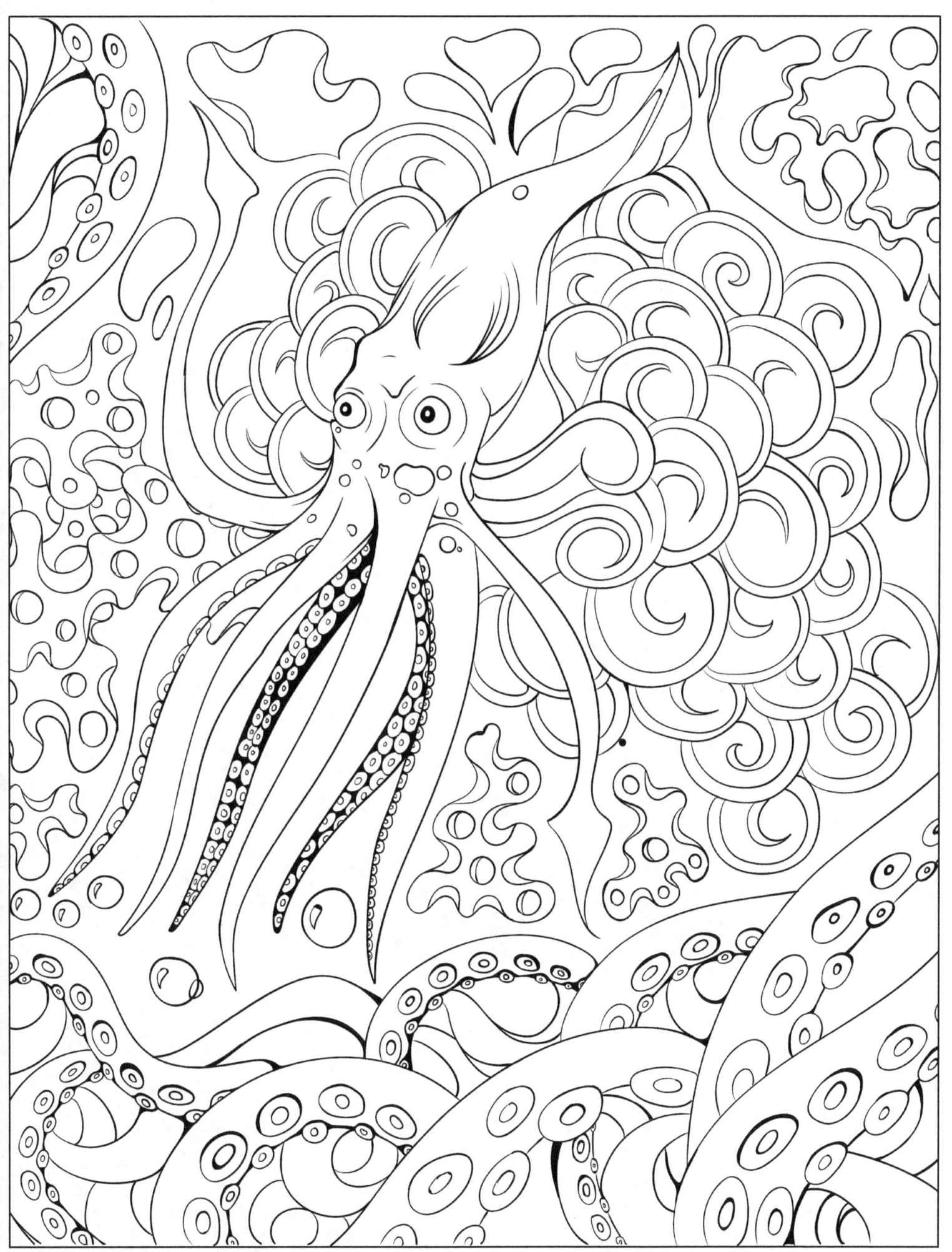

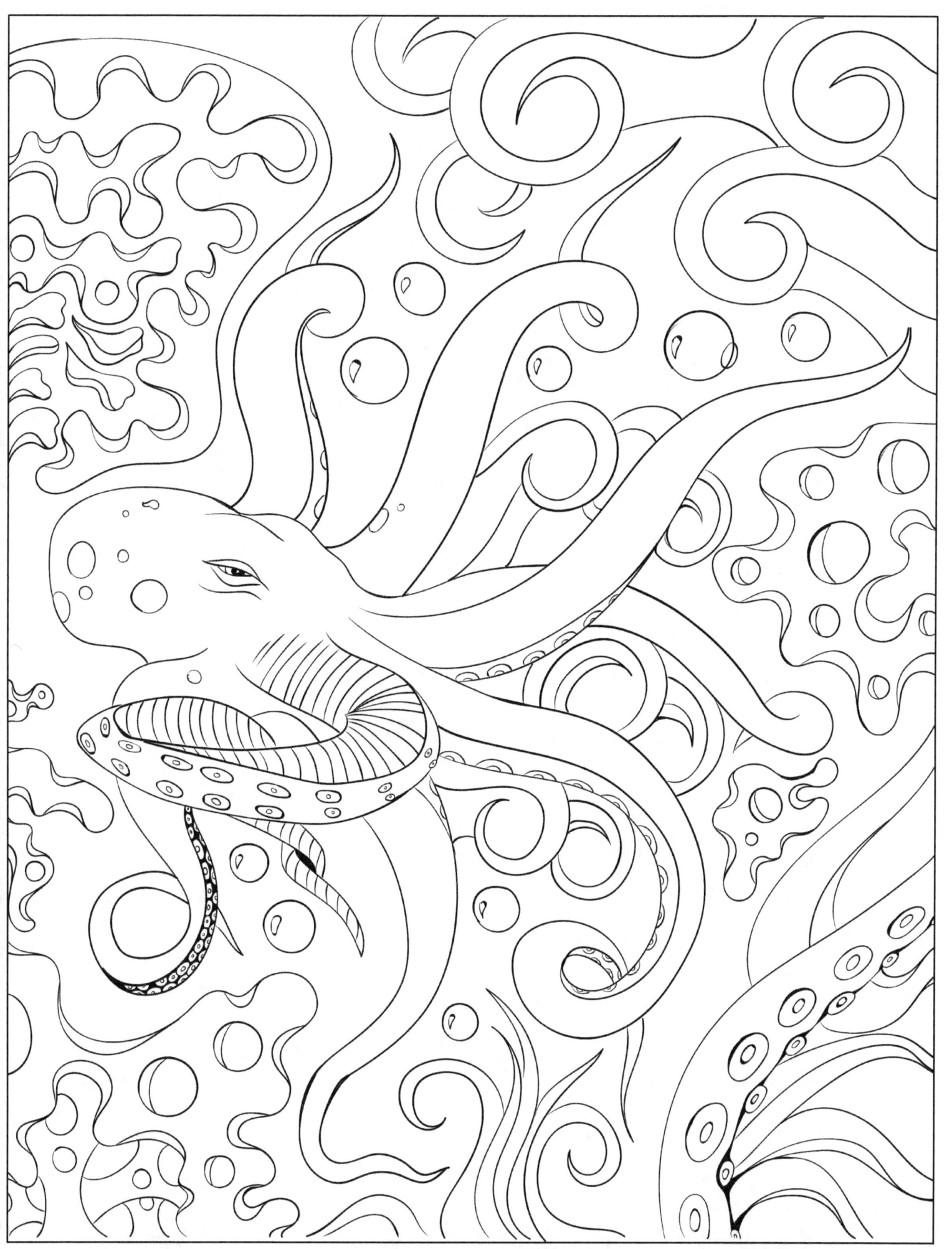

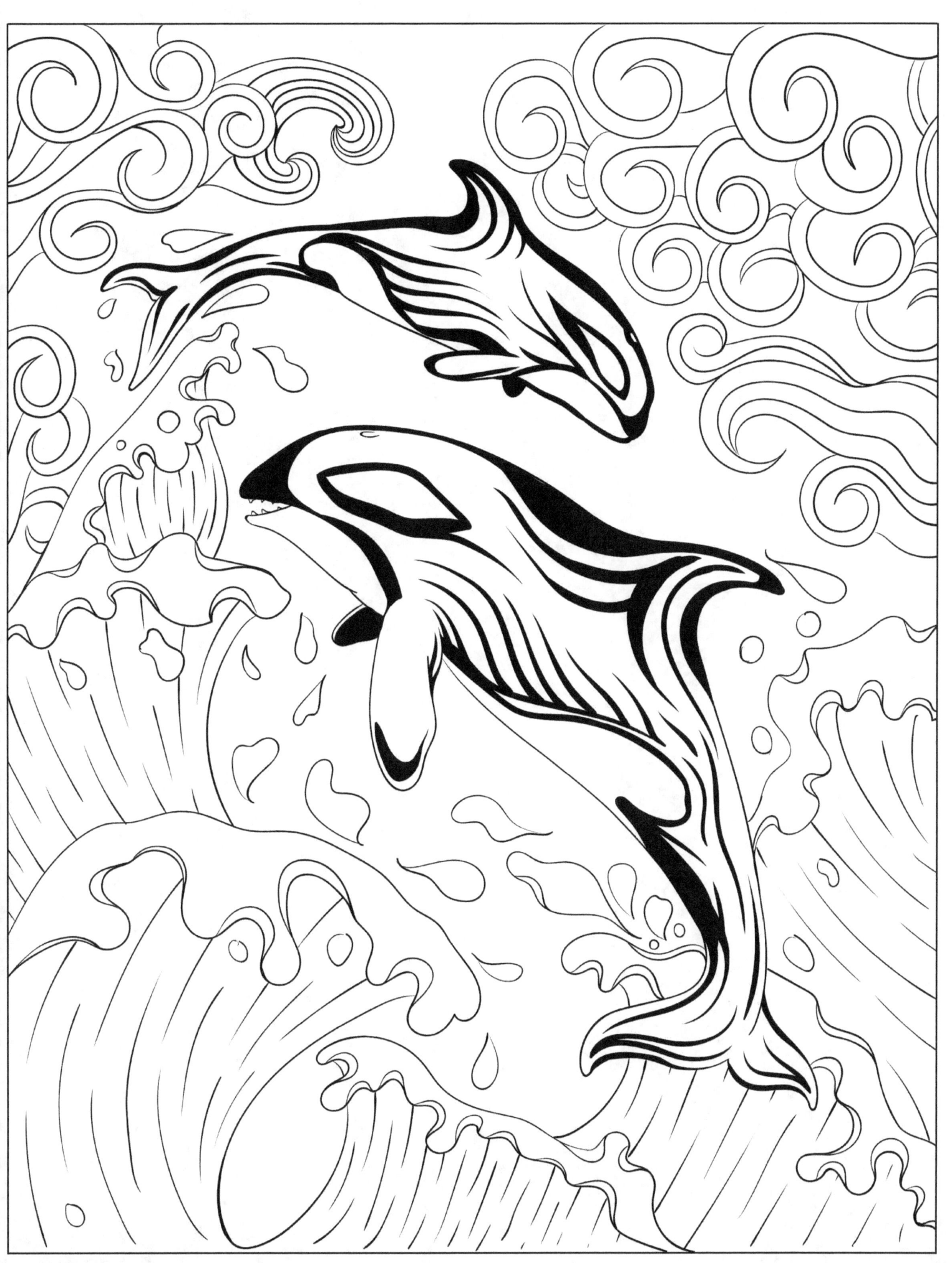

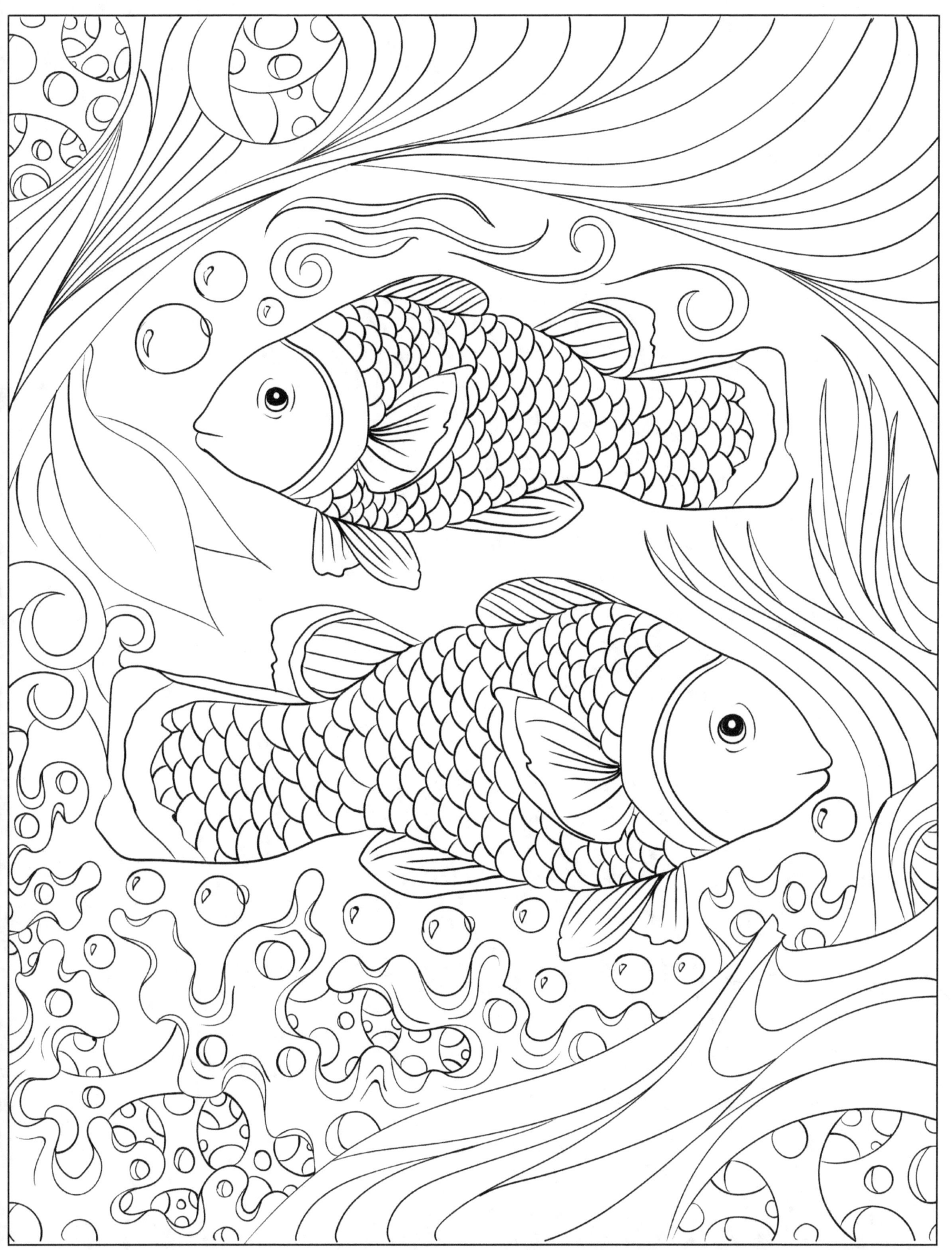

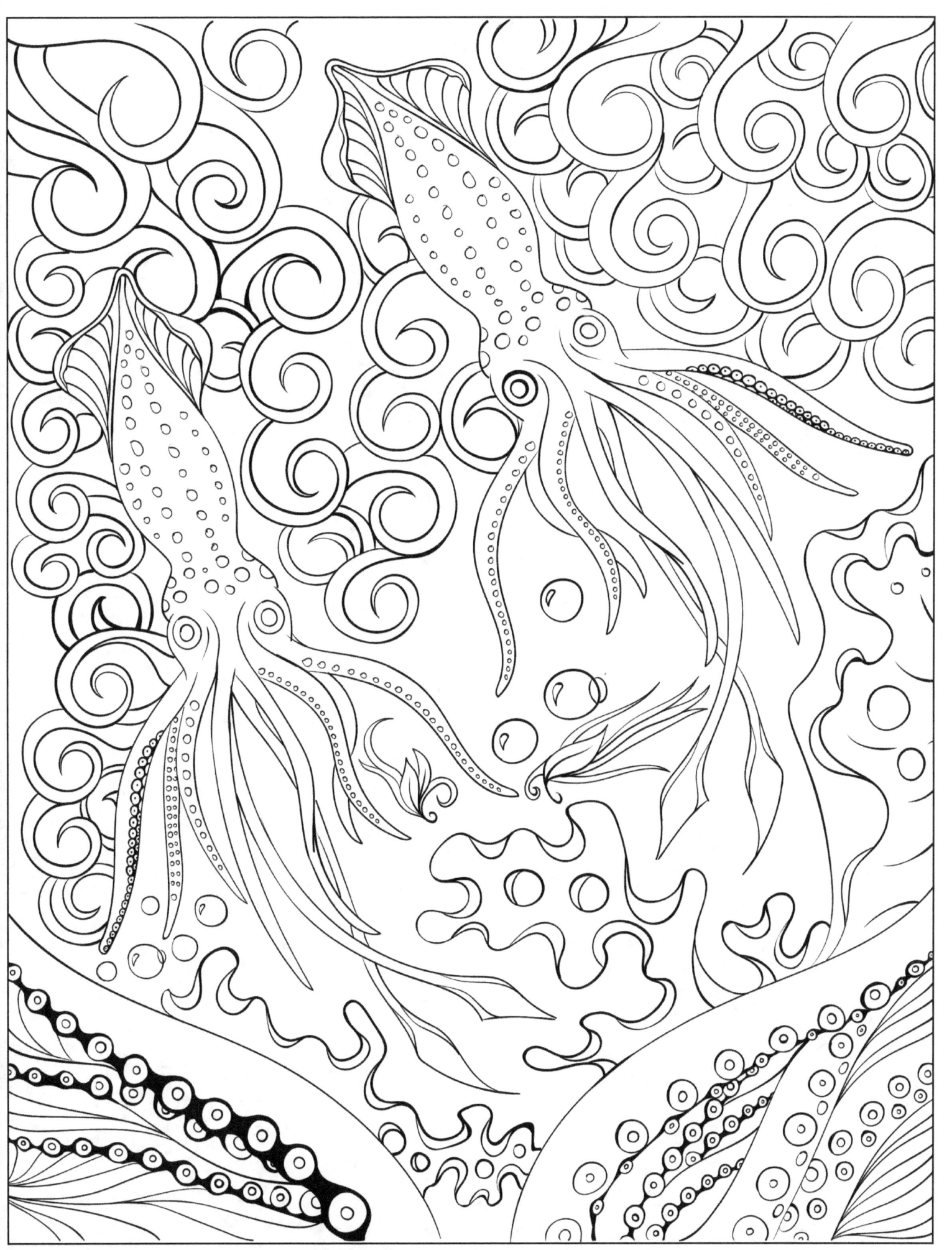

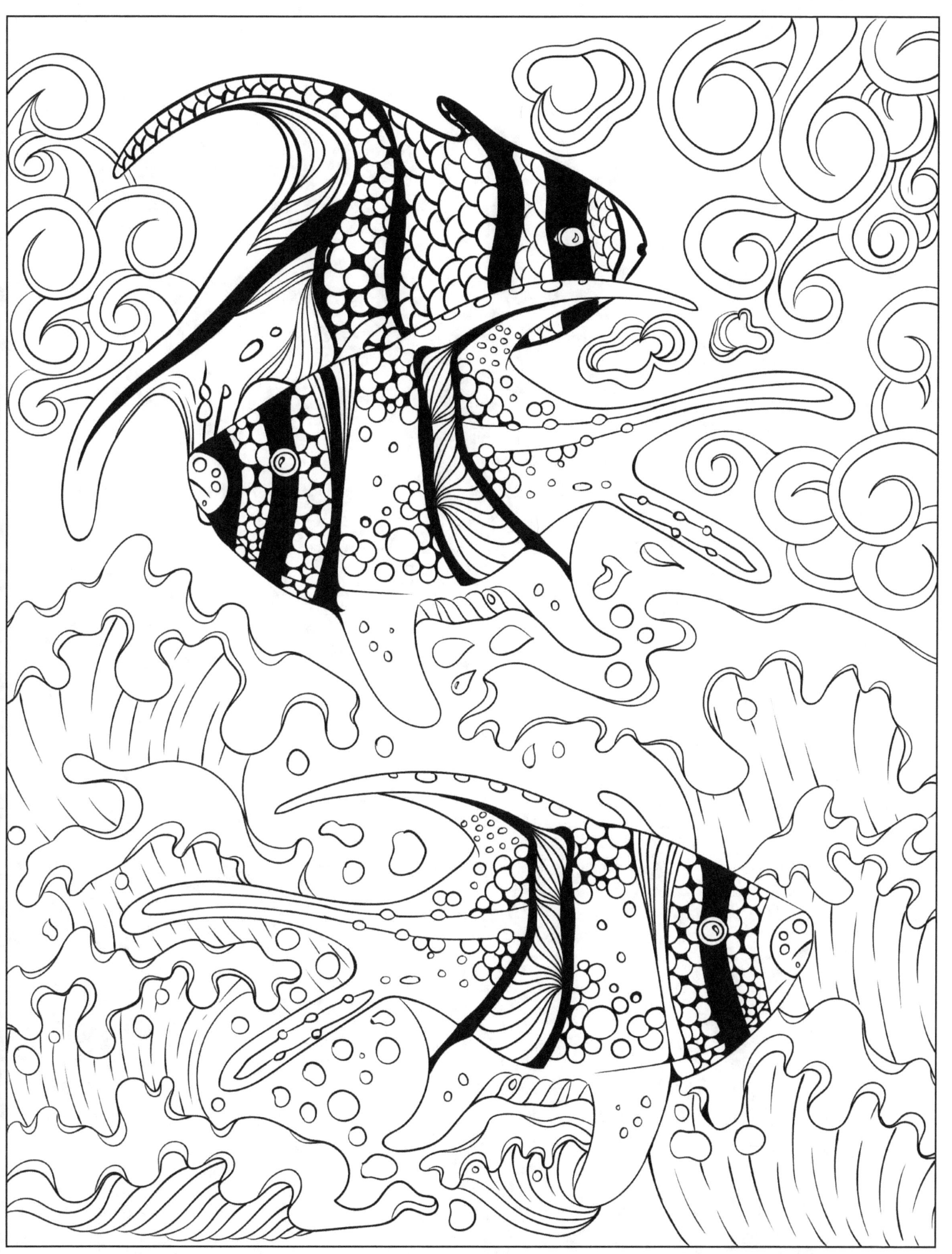

About The Author

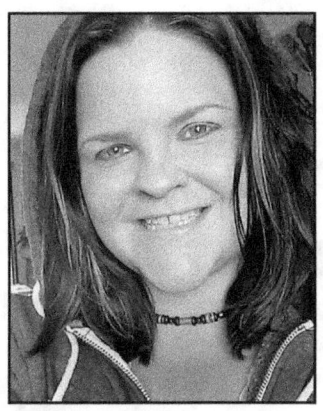

Kristy J Specht was born in Hastings, Minnesota in 1983. She first went to beauty school and obtained her cosmetology license and currently works as a hairstylist. She always enjoyed painting and sketching in her spare time and obtained her Associate's in Graphic Design in 2017. Having lost a few beloved pets over time (one recently in May 2016), she understands the bond between humans and animals and focuses her artwork around animals of all kinds; not just pets. It wasn't until late 2015 when she decided she wanted to publish her first Coloring Book after reading up on the trend and wanting to contribute her own work.

Other books:

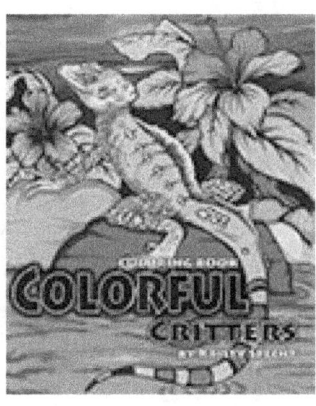

Colorful Critters: Coloring Book